D0031858

"A RARE AND TOUCHING BOOK,

one that acknowledges the daunting complexity of the parent-adolescent bond, while still providing hope, inspiration, and direction for mothers and their daughters. The author's capacity to blend real-life experience with timeless wisdom will serve to help both parent and child to navigate this rich and wondrous time while keeping their sanity, and their souls, intact."

—BRAD SACHS, PH.D.
Author of *The Good Enough Child: How to Have an Imperfect Family and Be Perfectly Satisfied*

"There is something for everyone here. . . . A great present for any mom or girl."

—CHERYL DELLASEGA
Author of *Surviving Ophelia*

"*The Mother-Daughter Circle,* like *Prayers on My Pillow,* is filled with heart warming stories accompanied by many welcome insights and wisdom. This book is an invitation for all mothers and their teenage daughters to experience the value of sharing and acceptance. As a mother-daughter psychotherapist team ourselves, we know how important it is to keep connections through the powerful teenage years. When this happens mothers and daughters are able to become adult friends and allies, connected by a bond of love and respect. May all women draw their circles large enough to include their mothers and daughters and in so doing may each woman and soon-to-be woman become their best selves. Celia Straus gives us all a boost in that direction."

—JULIE AND DOROTHY FIRMAN
Coauthors of *Chicken Soup for the Mother and Daughter Soul*

Praise for *The Mother-Daughter Circle*

"Celia Straus's work is groundbreaking. It seeks to introduce girls to their most authentic selves. Moms and daughters who follow Celia's guidelines will learn to create a rich, loving, *real* relationship that can last a lifetime."

—SUSAN PIVER BROWNE
Author of *The Hard Questions*

"If you didn't learn how to mother from *your* mother, learn from Celia Straus. She understands the needs of our youngest women in a deep and profound way."

—ROBIN RICE
Author of *A Hundred Ways to Sunday*

"Celia Straus has given mothers, and the daughters they love, a beautiful tool to grow even closer with her new book, *The Mother-Daughter Circle*. The exercises and ideas in this lovely little missive are wonderful prompts to strengthen the sacred connection between mother and daughter. Celia generously shares her own mothering stories as well as prayer/poems that cut to the essence of the typical teen's struggle. Buy this book for your daughter. Girls, buy this book for your mom!"

—MIMI DOE
Author of *Busy but Balanced* and
10 Principles for Spiritual Parenting
Founder of www.SpiritualParenting.com

"ONE OF THE MOST GENEROUS, JOYFUL, AND ABOVE ALL, HUMAN BOOKS ON PARENTING I HAVE EVER READ.

By making it possible for mothers to write in the book and then give it to their daughters, Celia Straus offers us the chance to be as wise and loving as she is. As the mother of a thirteen-year-old, I cannot thank her enough."

—JUDITH IVEY
Actress

"For all of the complexity that is typical in a mother-daughter relationship, this book, in the simplest of terms, personifies the power that exists between the two when they are able to make the right connection. . . . A beautifully written book."

—BONNIE W. MCDANIEL
Author of *In the Eye of the Storm: A Celebration of Family and the Real Purpose of Home*

"*The Mother-Daughter Circle* could just as easily apply to mothers and sons. There are many wise ways of connecting here for any mother to take to heart to foster a more loving relationship with her children."

—MAUREEN ORTH
Special Correspondent, *Vanity Fair*

"Much has been written about effective communication between mothers and daughters but seldom do authors focus on the everyday circumstances in which real change is possible. Until now."

— ROBYN WEGMAN

Margaret Taylor Smith Director of Women's Studies, Duke University

The Mother-daughter Circle

★ Celia Straus ★

To:

From:

I hold a secret in my heart
And the secret is love.
I hear a whisper in my ear
And the whisper is love.
I see a dream inside my mind
And the dream is love.
I take the gift life offers
And the gift is love.
I feel the warmth around me
And the warmth is love.

www.motherdaughtercircle.com

The
Mother-Daughter
Circle

The Mother-Daughter Circle

MAKING LIFELONG CONNECTIONS WITH YOUR TEENAGER

CELIA STRAUS

ILLUSTRATED BY
JULIA STRAUS

BALLANTINE BOOKS NEW YORK

A Ballantine Book
Published by The Ballantine Publishing Group

Copyright © 2003 by Celia Straus
Illustrations copyright © 2003 by Julia Straus

www.ballantinebooks.com

Book design by Nancy Singer Olaguera

Library of Congress Cataloging-in-Publication Data
Straus, Celia.
The mother-daughter circle : making lifelong connections with your teenager / Celia Straus ; illustrated by Julia Straus.—1st ed.
p. cm.
Includes bibliographical references.
ISBN 0-345-44886-3
1. Mothers and daughters. 2. Parent and teenager. I. Title.

HQ799.15 .S78 2003
306.874'3—dc21

2002028379

Manufactured in the United States of America

First Edition: April 2003

10   9   8   7   6   5   4   3   2   1

For the mothers and daughters of the world, my daughters, Julia and Emily, and my mother, Patricia.

And for Richard, my loving husband and devoted partner in parenting, who has supported and encouraged me throughout all our years together. His commitment to sustaining connections with our daughters based on mutual respect and love continues to be my inspiration.

Contents

Acknowledgments

$\mathcal{S}$oon after I had agreed to this project, it became apparent that writing *The Mother-Daughter Circle* was going to be a challenge. To begin with, I had a hunch that there were already numerous books published on the subject of mother-daughter relationships, adolescent girls, and spiritual parenting. It seemed critical to read as many of them as possible before I did anything else. During the winter, spring, and summer of 2001, I did my part to keep Amazon.com in business, and my hunch proved correct. There are an incredible number of authors writing inspiring books on the topics of spirituality, spiritual parenting, parenting, mother-daughter relationships, and adolescent girls, many of which I reference throughout this book.

I am especially indebted to works by Debra Whiting Alexander, Frederick and Mary Ann Brussat, June Cotner, Mimi Doe, Larry Dossey, M.D., Tilden Edwards, Julie and Dorothy Firman, Myla and Jon Kabat-Zinn, Madeleine L'Engle, Ann Tremaine Linthorst, Gerald G. May, M.D., Kathleen Norris, Hugh and Gayle Prather, Sharon Salzburg, Celeste Snowber Schroeder, Peg Streep, and Gary Zukav. I also found a wealth of wisdom and advice in these books: *Sacred Circles*, by Robin Carnes and Sally Craig; *Changes That Heal*, by Dr. Henry Cloud; *Beyond Nice: The Spiritual Wisdom of Adolescent*

Girls, by Patricia H. Davis; *Soul Prints*, by Marc Gafni; *Birth without Violence*, by Frederick Leboyer; *The Parent's Tao Te Ching*, by William Martin; and *A Quaker Book of Wisdom*, by Robert Lawrence Smith. I have listed these authors and many others in the back of the book.

I also spoke to many people who graciously shared their spiritual experiences and parenting knowledge with me. They are writers, healers, storytellers, mythmakers, psychotherapists, social workers, theologians, shamans, yoga and meditation instructors, priests, rabbis, producers, musicians, artists, and community activists. Many of them are mothers and fathers with preadolescent or adolescent daughters, and you'll be comforted to know that, no matter how wise or deeply spiritual they are, they all have approximately the same number of good and bad parenting days as the rest of us.

Therefore, my heartfelt thanks to Denise Baddour, Carolyn Bain, the Rev. Patricia Barrett, Heidi Berry, Ruth Blount, Joan Bramsch, Patricia Brim, Raymond Brim, Susan Piver Browne, Linda Chambers, Diane Collier, Julie Collins, the Rev. Carol Crumley, Christina Drukala, Nancy Eagleston, Dr. Mark Eig, Louise Garlock, Amy Gaver, Alexandra Gignoux, Beth Raebeck Hall, Pat Homeyer, Judith Ivey, Kimberly Jenkins, Lisa Kemp, Susan Koch, Judy Kovler, the Rev. Clark Lobenstine, Elizabeth Malloy, Cindy Martin, Joanne Mazurkl, Bonnie McDaniel, Allison McMillan-Lee, Dr. Gerald G. May, the Rev. Sandra Mayo, Sally Miller, Becky Mills, Joanne Mizurki, the Rev. Elizabeth Orens, Mary Preston, Travis Price, Gleaves Rhodes, Patience Robbins, Sue Rogers, Diane Sherwood, Jennifer Stockman, Nancy Vittrioni, and Valerie Zilinsky. I am humbled by your gifts of friendship and wisdom.

There are five more women who have provided me with their wisdom, enthusiasm, and knowledge of writing and publishing. One is my former editor, Joanne Wyckoff, who continues to offer her warm friendship, extraordinary sense of humor, and insight. My two editors at Ballantine during this project, Abby Durden and Allison Dickens, have been gracious guides through my first experience writing in complete sentences, intelligently and intuitively made suggestions crucial to the crafting of this book. My publicist, Cindy Murray, has been crucial to any success this book has. Finally, my literary agent, Sarah Jane Freymann, has, as always, been my source of motivation and balance, encouraging me to stretch and focus, and gently taking me to task when I enthused over a book idea better left undeveloped.

Yet even with all this support, I was still unable to conceptualize an approach to the book. I decided to post lengthy questionnaires about relationships between mothers and daughters on my Web site. The responses would serve as my field research. To my delight, hundreds of mothers and teenage girls patiently filled them out with a candor and grace I found extraordinary. Thank you. I hope many of you will recognize your words in this book, and that you will feel, as

I do, their resonance for others. *When I have quoted you, I have changed your names to protect the confidentiality of what you shared with me.*

I asked my mother to write about our relationship from the time I was born until I left for college, figuring that her perspective might jump-start the writing process. She responded with pages of detailed memories that were both literate and revealing. Mother, thank you for your loving support.

I spent long hours talking about the book and how to approach it with my husband, Richard, who listened patiently, offering his thoughts, suggestions, and insights as a parent, fellow writer, and sympathetic friend.

I asked my oldest daughter, Julia, if she would illustrate the book with pen and ink drawings. She said yes, and soon afterward drew an example of what she thought might work. It was perfect. I am so grateful, Julia, for your talent, your sense of whimsy, and your compassionate spirit. As always, you and your sister, Emily, are my guiding lights.

My family and friends finally grew tired of my excuses for not writing and stopped asking how I was doing. The summer of 2001 came and went. School started. And then the tragic events of September 11 occurred. With the rest of the world, our family sat glued to the television set. At some point during those first terrible hours of images of mass destruction, my daughters confronted me, saying, "You are always telling us to trust in God's divine plan for us. How could this horror be part of that plan?" They weren't just feeling vulnerable; they felt angry and betrayed.

Both my husband and I had spoken to them, aware of other terrible events in the history of mankind demonstrating evil on such a grand scale that was part of the human condition. But we had also said that these events were lessons they should learn from, yet would not have to experience, not now, not here. We had been proven wrong, and I had no reassuring answers for them. My faith was as shaken as theirs.

Days later I found a valid reason to put off solving the problem of how to write *The Mother-Daughter Circle*. I was asked to do research (I write training and documentary videos) and interviewing for American Red Cross Disaster Services. The job required several days in New York City at various Red Cross disaster operations sites, including the Respite Center for workers at Ground Zero.

At Ground Zero, hundreds of men and women, from firefighters, police, FBI, and National Guard to construction workers, were coming from "the pile" to the Respite Center around the clock for food, rest, and emotional support. In talking with them, I was impressed, not only by the magnitude of their grief and exhaustion, but also by their determination to persevere; to accept the unthinkable. In order to do so, these people wanted to connect with one another out of a need to give and receive love. The support they most valued, that most successfully met their needs, that brought these committed yet distraught men and women dressed in work boots and overalls covered with dust back again and again to the Respite Center for, well, *respite,* was a connection—the offer of common ground.

Repeatedly I was told by those staffing the respite center—mental health workers, a priest, a massage therapist, a mass care cafeteria worker—that the best way to meet the needs of those seeking respite was to simply be there to listen and accept. Red Cross volunteers spent most of their time just hanging out, being open and friendly with no personal agendas, no preconceived strategies, and no "one size fits all" approaches. In other words, the same connections that work in a parent-child relationship, such as flexibility, listening, nonjudgmental acceptance, honesty, and openness, worked here as well. Moreover, the Red Cross disaster services volunteers with whom I spoke all agreed that they had never felt so needed, so satisfied, and so fulfilled.

Little "communities of spirit" sprang up spontaneously. There were no leaders in these groups, only participants. No teachers; only learners. People treated one another with dignity, respect, and *compassion*. The underlying theme of the books I had read, and the answers of e-mailed questionnaires I had retrieved were being demonstrated in stark relief all around me. Of course that was not all that was going on, but that is the part I remember best. And so I thank the Red

Cross Mass Care, Mental Health and Spiritual Care staff, and all the men and women who were working at Ground Zero as well as all who visited Respite Center One for demonstrating the strength and purpose of spiritual connections.

And so I returned home with an answer for my daughters and an approach to this book. I was more certain than ever of God's love and its presence within and around us. I had seen evidence of it in the days I spent in New York. During the next few weeks I hugged my girls and my husband and told them I loved them as often as they would let me. I listened more and talked less. Through my actions, I tried to communicate to them an appreciation of the ephemeral nature of life and the importance of rejoicing in the moment. Thank you, Richard, Julia, and Emily, for giving me the opportunity to love you and for teaching me how to awaken to the wonder of our lives together.

The
Mother-Daughter
Circle

Connecting with Spirit

I Am Beautiful. Look at Me.

I am intelligent. Listen carefully.
I am faithful. Tell me all.
I am steadfast. Dare to fall.
I am giving. Ask away.
I am loving. Dare to stay.
I am funny. Share my smile.
I am patient. Stay a while.
I am courageous. Trust my heart.
I am gentle. Come apart.
I am playful. Try my game.
I am waiting. Call my name.

MORE PRAYERS ON MY PILLOW

*T*his is a book about making connections with ourselves and with our daughters through the spiritual in our lives, a common meeting ground where relationships blossom and thrive. Moreover, the book itself is a connection. It is written to be personalized by you, and then given to your daughter as a way of showing your love, acceptance, and celebration of who she is. When direct communication with each other is in meltdown, an indirect approach often works. Sharing thoughts about yourself and your relationship with her, rebuilds mutual trust and respect.

For me, the challenge in connecting with my two teenage daughters has often been knowing what I want to say, but not knowing how to say it (like my initial dilemma with this book). If you're asking yourself, *"Is that my problem?"* take this quick quiz to find out:

You stand in front of the bedroom door she has just slammed in your face. In the past you would have simply opened the door, gone into your thirteen-year-old daughter's room, and resolved the argument then and there. A few more angry words, sure, some tears, of course, but ultimately an embrace and cuddle before she went to sleep. What has happened? Because now you:

  A. Tap gently on the door and ask if she's okay even though she has just declared that you have ruined

her life and is sobbing. You wait, frozen in time,
wondering why she doesn't answer.

B. Throw open the door, stride in and, in your best au-
thoritarian tone, announce that she is never to shut
her door in your face again, and that going to a
girl-boy party at Gretchen's house when her parents
are out of town is not an option, nor will it ever be.

C. Calmly but sternly say, through the door, that you've
had it with these screaming matches. She can stay in
there until the cows come home, as far as you're
concerned. You're going to bed (but not to sleep).

D. Do all of the above

E. Do none of the above. There is an alternative: The
connections you have sustained together can be re-
lied on, now, to resolve this conflict and leave you
both feeling closer than you did before the argument
started.

Well, naturally, E is the response we're looking for, but,
personally, there are still plenty of times I respond with
A, B, C, or D to my fourteen-year-old. The challenge of
communicating with our daughters about *anything*, much
less about intimate feelings and innermost needs, can be
daunting:

"I know I shouldn't yell at her. It doesn't solve anything. And I hate the sound of my voice when I'm doing it. But I can't help myself. She pushes my buttons!"

mother of eleven-year-old

"I wish I could get rid of this anxiety that just nags at me all day because I should—no, make that *must*—talk to my daughter about sex now that she is maturing, but I'm afraid to. What if I say the wrong thing and she never confides in me again?"

mother of fourteen-year-old

And, guess what (no surprise here)? Your daughter faces the same challenge:

"I can't talk to my mother about my personal problems because I can't make her understand."

Angie, age 11

"I wish I could talk to my mom about sex and boys, but I don't know how to start."

Brittany, age 13

"I want to talk to her about boys and kissing and stuff, but what do I say?"

Kelly, age 14

"I can't talk to my mother about my feelings."

Pat, age 16

"I've never been able to talk to my mother. I just talk to my friends."

Janine, age 14

One of the greatest challenges of parenting is choosing constructive responses that strengthen our relationships with our children. Instead, we fall back into old patterns of behavior that we know won't work, but repeat anyway. As women, daughters, and mothers, we have had a lot of conditioning. Our conditioning is one of the maps we use to journey through motherhood. The spiritual in our lives is another map, but a less familiar one for many of us.

This book is for all of us who are in the process of discovering how spirit can guide our journey, but who may be slow learners. I'm the tortoise, not the hare. I learn best through experience. And, until 1982, when my first daughter, Julia, was born, my experience with spirituality was pretty much limited to going to Episcopal services, and having discussions with Richard, my husband, who is Jewish, about whether or not to have a Christmas tree. It was not until twelve years later, when Julia was going through the turmoil of her preteen years, that I became aware of what was missing in our lives. After that, it took me another year of writing a different prayer every night for my daughter in an effort to help *her* discover how spirituality could be a guide for *her* journey through adolescence, in order to learn about *my* spirituality. So I probably should add that I'm a very slow tortoise.

We can love, guide, support, and protect our daughters. Ultimately they will, however, live out their destinies with God's presence working through them. So, if we can also connect through spirit, we can enhance their inner selves as well as our own.

Ok, let's be practical. Take a deep breath, relax, and let our relationships with our daughters heal and grow. As one mother e-mailed, "I am so tired of being called 'weird' by my twelve-year-old. Is this going to be her only response to what I have to say for the next eight years?" If you are like me, rather than simply wait for her to "grow out of it," you would like to try another way of relating that will help both of you feel better about each other and yourselves *right now*.

This book is about discovering those moments when we connect with each other and then finding ways to make them happen more often.

We all have these moments:

> "Sometimes my daughter and I will be driving along and we'll see something odd going on and we'll both, at the exact same moment, turn to each other and say something like, 'Whoa,' or, 'Pretty strange.' I know that's a little thing, but it's reassuring to share the same reaction."
>
> *mother of sixteen-year-old*

> "I remember a time when she was really upset [about] not making the soccer team and I just sat there stroking her hair and holding her like I did when she was little, and for some reason I started singing a song I used to sing to her before she went to bed. It's called 'Green Grow the Lilacs.' "
>
> *mother of fourteen-year-old*

> "Our best times together are when we're watching a video on my bed, and my daughters are curled up beside me."
>
> *mother of two girls, ages 10 and 13*

"We make waffles or pancakes together on Sunday morning. It's just us in the kitchen and we talk the whole time."

mother of eleven-year-old

"My favorite times with my mom are when we talk on her bed or watch TV and veg."

Polly, age 12

"I like it when we go shopping together or just drive around. That's when I feel closest to her."

Margaret, age 15

"We get our nails done together or we bake. That's my time with my mom."

Rachel, age 13

"My mom and I go shopping and we act like little kids."

Tammy, age 14

We can look for times when, together with our daughters, we are simply being *in spirit*, honoring each other's individuality and unique presence. We can practice trusting that our lives will unfold according to God's plan no matter what we do. We can repeat these connections and experience the benefits they offer. They fill us with positive energy, provide relaxation, enthusiasm, and laughter, and detach us from our personal agendas. The more we let these connections happen, the more often they happen. The more we experience the feeling of love that comes with each connection, the more we are able to connect again, receiving love and giving it back. *The Mother-Daughter Circle* is as much about connecting with your spirit as it is about connecting with your daughter's. Our connections encircle us; as the poet Rainer Maria Rilke observed: "There is nothing so wise as a circle."

Applying the concepts in this book requires no talent, no great mothering skills, no preparation, no formal religion unless you practice one, which is also fine, no advanced educational degrees. Connecting with spirit is about letting things happen. There are places in the book for you to stop reading, let your thoughts occur, and jot them down.

In other words, please personalize what I have written. It's as if we were having a chat that I started, but you were also responding to by saying things like, "Yes, I can relate to that. I remember when she'd just turned four and . . ." Or, "Yes, yes! I know *exactly* what you mean. The same thing happened to me when . . ." Or, "You think *that's* pathetic, listen to this. . . ."

Most importantly, I urge you to give this book to your daughter. At some point, when you have read enough and written enough—and you'll know when that point is—offer it to her. Your daughter may not read a word I wrote, but she will read everything you wrote. And when she responds, it will be because you have given her the greatest gift you have to offer—yourself, the most important woman in her life.

Connection

Why is it so difficult to trust you?
Why is it so impossible to care?
Why, when your warmth is offered, am I frozen?
Why, when you reach out, am I not there?

Why, though every day I wake up lonely,
And waking, search for love I cannot find,
Am I unable to return your smile,
So afraid you'll see into my mind?

Why have I built walls I will not scale
When I'm so desperately seeking a way out?
My world is locked. I've lost the combination
I'm safe inside, but what else have I got?

Please help me find just one connection through my spirit
To all the joy that life is meant to be.
Please start with just the simplest of gestures
By offering a part of you to me.

MORE PRAYERS ON MY PILLOW

Connecting Since Birth

The Night That You Were Born

The night that you were born, as the clock struck seven
You came into this world, a gift from heaven.
And all the nurses laughed, for your face was smiling
To be here on the earth and be so beguiling.
They say you had dimples where the angels kissed you
As tokens of their love and to show they'd miss you.
And you were blessed with life, a new soul parting
The night that you were born, purest love just starting.

PRAYERS ON MY PILLOW

As parents, and friends, of children, we may take part in birthing our children, but they are here to birth something far more profound in us: the eyes to see as a child again. It's not easy to see with a child's eyes, so we are given the opportunity through our children. We are sent the bread of angels to experience the heart of God.

IN THE WOMB OF GOD, BY CELESTE SNOWBER SCHROEDER

"When I saw my daughter for the first time, I was completely unprepared for what I would feel. It was such joy."

mother of thirteen-year-old

"We went to get her at the orphanage. I was extremely stressed out. I had waited so long for this moment, but I was also afraid. I didn't know what I was going to feel, and that made me nervous. But when I saw her, I just melted. I still melt."

mother of adopted ten-year-old from Colombia

"Whenever I get really angry at Monica, I try to think back on the last time I breast-fed her. I had to go back to work, and she took to the bottle. It didn't make sense to continue. But I remember looking down and loving her so much and thinking this part is going to stop now, and I started crying. I got her little face all wet with my tears. So when I get mad, I think about how I felt then."

mother of eleven-year-old

"I remember the birth of every one of my girls, and each time, for me, it was like what I imagine looking at the face of God would be."

mother of five girls, ages 8 to 25

"I chose home birthing because I wanted to welcome her into the world in the most loving and gentle way I could think of."

mother of fifteen-year-old

"One of my favorite times is when my mom talks about how it was when she gave birth to me. I just love to hear her talk about that."

Sara, age 12

"My mom's pregnant-with-me stories are hysterical."
Alexis, age 17

"Sometimes I ask my mother to tell me everything about when I was born."
Michelle, age 15

"I love it when I'm sick and she stays up and comforts me by telling me stories about when I was little."
Chanie, age 13

"My mother says she played the piano the whole time I was in her tummy. I think that is why I like music better than anything."
Rebecca, age 9

*W*hen my daughters and I share stories, our favorites are about how they were born. If I forget something, like the name of the movie my husband and I were watching when I started having contractions when pregnant with Julia (*Victor/Victoria*), or how Emily was fed for the first three days with an eyedropper, they remind me. Julia's story chronicles an anxiety-free, "glowing" first pregnancy culminating with the delivery of a plump eight-and-a-half-pound baby girl.

Emily's story is quite the opposite. It is about a risky pregnancy, some of which was spent in bed, culminating almost two months early with a C-section and delivery of a scrawny, four-pound baby girl. I tell them other stories about the often humorous ways I met the challenges of first-time motherhood. There was the time I took Julia in a portable bassinet to a local restaurant, was seated at a booth, stored her safely away under the table, where she went to sleep, and then completely forgot about her. Luckily, the appalled waiter noticed before I left. However, their birthing stories make the strongest connections, because in each telling, we experience, *together,* an awareness of the first mother-daughter bond.

Our birthing stories are personal myths filled with adventure and wonder. In each telling we feel the essential mystery of life. I describe how, when I held them close as infants, I was filled with a deep contentment and love. The quality of my experience was intense because, for the moment, I was completely aware that this was the exact and only place we needed to be, my baby daughter and I. I felt in tune with life. My daughter connects with me *during* the telling. Why? She was one of two heroines in the story.

So let's continue to share our birthing stories. It does not have to be the whole story. Your story may be an action-packed adventure, like my friend Joy's, who gave birth to her daughter while sitting backward in the passenger seat of her Jeep Wrangler at night in a rainstorm as she instructed her friend, who until that night had never driven a stick shift, on how to drive. Or, you may want to describe a more peaceful moment:

OUR BIRTH MOMENT WAS WHEN . . .

Communicating with our children often begins before they are born. While life forms inside our wombs, we speak monologues reflecting a wide range of emotions from overwhelming love and joyous anticipation to occasional anger and resentment. When I was pregnant with Emily, a routine sonogram during my second trimester showed a prematurely aging placenta, which put her at grave risk. I was sent to bed to spend the last months of my pregnancy in solitude. I was forced to surrender into myself, allowing God to grow and shape my daughter. For a person who took pride in multitasking and efficient use of time, it was a challenge to learn to be patient, to allow life to happen instead of trying to control it.

Without voicing a word, I found myself in continuous conversation with my daughter, encouraging her to grow and thrive. We were partners, I'd tell her, teammates working on the lung development project together. When I ate a sandwich, I asked her how she liked it. When I heard a song from one of my favorite rock groups, I promised her that later on she'd get to see, for example, Creedence Clearwater Revival performing "Who'll Stop the Rain?" We were soul mates in the most literal sense.

What kinds of conversations did you carry on with your daughter during your pregnancy? Did you have a pet name for your little soul mate? A particular prayer? A favorite song or lullaby? How did you connect with someone you'd never seen but already loved?

I FIRST COMMUNICATED WITH YOU BEFORE YOU
WERE BORN BY . . .

"The child is between two worlds. On a threshold. Hesi-
tating. Do not hurry. Do not press. Allow this child to enter."
Sounds like some wise poet's parenting advice for a young
girl about to begin her adolescence, doesn't it? She's betwixt
and between, so let her experience this passage without med-
dling. It's not. This passage is from *Birth without Violence*,
Frederick Leboyer's landmark book about the way we bring
children into the world. Basically, he urges us to consider
birth from the baby's point of view, telling us that newborns
are fully aware humans, wise and knowing. Here's some
more familiar-sounding advice from Leboyer: "This is an elusive, ephemeral moment. Leave this child. Alone. Because
this child is free. Stay back. Let time pass. Grant this mo-

ment its slowness, and its gravity." Isn't that exactly how we *wish* we could behave with our ten-year-old on the verge of puberty?

"I remember quietly watching Leonora as she tried on her older sister's party dress and heels. She was so serious, so intent as she looked at herself in the mirror, studying, posing. She is no longer a little girl playing dress up, but she isn't sixteen, either. I'm so glad I was able to leave without her seeing me. I'll always remember how she looked."

mother of eleven-year-old

"I'll never forgive myself for dismissing out of hand— almost laughing, really—when Annie asked if I would buy her a bra. She looked so hurt."

mother of twelve-year-old

The advice in Leboyer's book, first published in 1974 in France, is absolutely relevant to mothering our teenage daughters today. Throughout *Birth without Violence*, Leboyer talks to mothers about staying relaxed, creating an atmosphere of tranquillity for the newborn, breathing deeply to stay centered and connected to oneself and one's child. We honor the newborn child as a unique and completely perfect individual and, most important, we trust in Nature. "How does Nature make smooth this transition?" he asks. "Very simply. Nature is a strict mother, but a loving one. We misunderstand her intentions, then we blame her for what follows. Everything about this event is arranged by Nature so that both leap and landing are made as easy as possible."

Coping with leaps and landings is what mothering is all about, whether our children are babies or teenagers. And we are capable of coping—particularly if we release the way we were conditioned to cope, those mindless knee-jerk reactions, and pause to reflect on how we might cope in a more spiritual way. Instead of trying to micromanage our daughters' leaps—"I can't believe you are freaking out because I got my belly button pierced"—and landings—"You don't know why all the girls hate me now, because even I don't know why"—we might simply open our hearts and trust a little more in the nurturing, loving, and always supportive God.

Leboyer points out that "every child must pass through the same stages leading from an enclosed world to an open one, from being folded inward to reaching outward. Each child travels this path in its own manner. And we should not always assume that those who travel most easily will fare the best." He describes babies who "bound into life, then suddenly withdraw into their own anger"; babies who struggle, incapable of escaping their own fears, and babies who emerge "casually, barely uttering a cry." Isn't this exactly how we might describe our daughters as they enter puberty? Each one has her own temperament and individual responses to life. And isn't our acceptance of their essential goodness the only way we can be lovingly present in their lives?

"She was such a noisy little munchkin. The doctor didn't have to do a thing to get her to cry. I remember her little face all squinched up. And then it seemed like she didn't *stop* crying for the next four months."

mother describing her firstborn

"Now my third one, she was just about effortless. I'm not complaining, mind you. They were telling me to push almost as soon as I got the hospital gown on. And before I knew it, there she was. It was definitely what you would call a natural childbirth. My littlest angel. She still is."

mother of three girls

> "I don't want to think about it. I love my daughter more than anything in the world, but I still can't believe what I went through to have her. No one prepared me for that. But then, no one prepared me for her adolescence, either."
>
> *mother of thirteen-year-old*

Here is how my mother describes my entrance into this world:

You were a high instrument delivery. I had been in labor for nearly twenty-four hours, but you still just didn't want to be born. You were extremely stubborn. Dr. Wherritt insisted on bringing you out naturally but said afterward he'd never had such a tug to pull a baby out. When I first saw you, you were badly swollen around your eyes and forehead, and purple, green, and yellow from the forceps. I was so worried. The nurse promised me that would go away.

Thank goodness the nurse was right. But the "extremely stubborn" part has not changed. I am as determined and bullheaded as anyone I know. Did your mother share her birthing experience with you? Have you told her story to your daughter? If you know nothing about how your daughter's grandmother birthed you, that's interesting in itself.

WHEN YOUR GRANDMOTHER GAVE BIRTH TO ME . . .

Now, take a moment to tell your daughter about some little quirk or personality trait she exhibited as a newborn that made you smile.

YOU HAD THIS WAY OF . . .

Share a memory of the way the two of you related as baby and mother:

OUR FIRST CONNECTIONS WERE WHEN . . .

Is there anything about how the two of you relate to each other years later that is reminiscent of the way you related when she was a baby?

WE STILL . . .

. . . THE SAME WAY WE DID WHEN YOU WERE A BABY.

If we are conscious of how we connected with our newborn, we can create that same connection during her adolescent years. How we connected with spirit in the beginning can work for a lifetime.

Take, for example, touching. When Julia was an infant, I would walk around holding her, gently rubbing her back to calm her when she was crying. Now that Julia is a young adult, I still occasionally rub her back, particularly when words do not work. It connects us. At nineteen, late in the evening, when she was home from college for the first time, she lay down on the bed next to me and said, "Mommy, rub my back."

Our childbirth expert, Leboyer, talks about "touching our babies with loving hands." This could apply to all interactions with our children, not just how we touch our newborns. We cherish moments when we are attentive and loving to our children and they open up their hearts to us. Unfortunately, there are also occasions when we are rigid, hostile, and unaware of the impact on our daughters.

"I've given up trying to talk to my mom, because she's always away at work and when she's home, she's too stressed out. I talk to my friends."

Ronda, age 14

"I would be afraid to talk to my parents about how I feel, because they get angry at me about doing chores and stuff, so think how they'd get if I talked to them about sex and boys."

Kim, age 14

> "I used to talk to my mother, but now I don't as much. She just wants to lecture me."
>
> *Carolyn, age 15*

> "We never hug anymore."
>
> *Rosalinda, age 15*

How might we touch our daughters? Leboyer would answer, "With hands that are attentive, alive, alert, and responsive. Hands that are light. That neither command nor demand. That are simply there." Gestures of love that bring us into physical contact with our daughters, particularly if verbal communication has broken down, establish common ground. Whether we hug, rub, stroke, caress, or cuddle, touching connects us to each other and our essential selves.

> "My mother pulls me into her lap when I'm sad, and it makes me feel better."
>
> *Sarah, age 18*

"She gives me a hug and puts her chin on my head."

Amanda, age 12

"She scratches my back and cuddles with me like I am still a little kid."

Lucia, age 11

"My mom runs her fingers across my forehead."

Jacqueline, age 16

"I love it when my mother lets me lay my head on her shoulder while we are watching a movie or TV."

Laura, age 18

"Sometimes we do stupid stuff, like I'll grab my mother's hand and go, 'We gued (I mean 'glue,' but I couldn't say it when I was little) together forever.' Something I did when I was little when I promised her I'd never leave her."

Suzi, age 17

There are plenty of ways to be more attentive and comforting through touch. It helps to remember how we touched our daughters as babies. How did you soothe your daughter through touch when she was a baby?

WHEN YOU WERE A BABY I USED TO . . .

And how would you soothe her now?

NOW I . . .

But what if our daughters do not want to be touched? We reach out to hug them and they freeze, flinch, and withdraw.

"I would like to be more affectionate with my daughter, but she shrugs me off. It didn't used to be like that."

mother of thirteen-year-old

"Well, she never allows me to hug her in front of her friends, but if I don't come in to kiss her good night, she wants to know if I'm angry at her."

mother of eleven-year-old

What do we do to connect with our babies when they have grown up and no longer want to be held? With a little trust in our feelings of connectedness at their birth, we can follow Leboyer's advice and have "hands that are light. That neither command nor demand." We are "simply there." We can touch, not physically, but with spirit.

"I just wait. I don't add anything. I let whatever we've said hang there. And then, after a while, we start talking again."

mother of sixteen-year-old

"My favorite times with my mom are when we walk to the ice-cream shop and get milk shakes even when it is snowing outside. Sometimes we walk the whole way without saying a word to each other, but we both know what the other one is thinking."

Hillary, age 13

"I know she understands more than I think. She knows how I feel without me saying a word. In fact, if I can just *zip my lips* and keep silent, it usually turns out okay. It usually turns out better."

mother of ten-year-old

Think of a time when you touched your daughter by letting her simply "be." Remember how it felt when she was a baby and loving her was all you *could* do. Perhaps you just listened to her without saying a word. You simply waited, trusting that whatever she said or did not say, whether she responded or not, it would be okay.

I FEEL WE CONNECT WITHOUT TOUCHING WHEN I . . .

From our newborn daughters' perspective, we *were* their world, and together we relished those moments when we could linger in the here and now. There was no miscommunication, because no words were needed. Connection was simple because it involved the mutual respect that comes when two people share the same understanding, knowing, and feeling. And, although we may not have been able to sustain this first connection over a long period of time, it still runs deep.

For She Is There to Care for Me

Her very soul I'll touch.
And she will smile
As she did when
We were as one, for now, as then
My mother loves me much.

MORE PRAYERS ON MY PILLOW

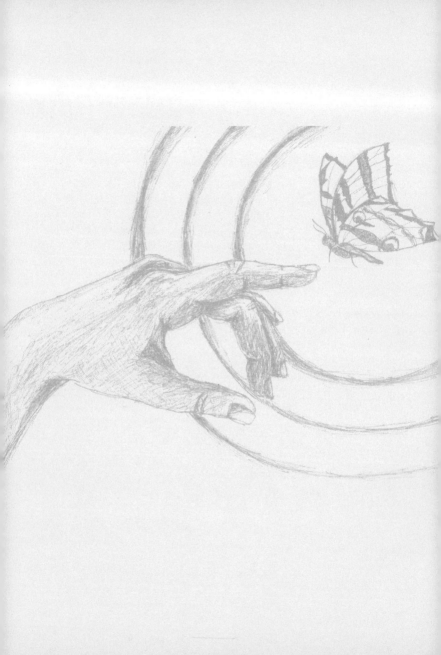

TWO

Connecting in the Moment

May I Take This Moment

To listen to my self
Turn off mind's chatter
Silence the voice
That interrupts prayers
And hear the rush
Of spirit's release.
May the soft sweet murmur
Of childhood's singing
Reach down deep
Into regions unknown
And find love waiting
To show me the way.

MORE PRAYERS ON MY PILLOW

When I am with my daughter, I have practiced being in the moment and sensing all that is around me. I have delighted in making mud soup, searching for worms, watching and laughing as a pet bunny rabbit hops around the yard, dancing in the warm rain. She has shown me how to receive what is, rather than focusing on a need to accomplish or produce something.

"THE CALL TO SPIRITUAL GROWTH IN PARENTHOOD,"
SHALEM NEWS, 1997, BY PATIENCE ROBBINS

"The one mistake I make repeatedly as a mom is not taking time to be with my daughter. Days go by and we won't have a single conversation, just the two of us. I know I'm going to regret it when she leaves for college next year, but I can't seem to do anything about it."

mother of eighteen-year-old

"Last night my daughter asked if she could model her prom dress for me, and I said, 'Later, I'm on an important call.' When I got off, she'd gone on to something else. I could have cut the phone call short. It wasn't all that important."

mother of sixteen-year-old

"I try to be available for her anytime. Answering *any* question. Being her friend *and* her mom. Trying to not control her life."

mother of fifteen-year-old

"When we walk our dogs, my daughter and I always have a good time because all we're concentrating on is being the owners of three crazy terriers, Saki, Sophy, and Sam."

mother of ten-year-old

"My mom and my sister and I were watching *Friends* and something happened that made us laugh so hard that snot came out my nose, and I thought, gosh, I sure hope we all remember this the next time we're fighting."

Lisa, one of two twins, age 13

"The best times with my mother are when we are just hanging out together and doing nothing."

Pilar, age 11

"My mother lets me talk without interrupting me to give her opinion."

Abby, age 12

"When my mom and I are in the car driving someplace and an old rock song comes on the radio, we both sing along. That's my favorite moment."

Debbie, age 13

*B*eing in the moment is, literally, as simple as breathing: Take a deep breath and, as you fill your lungs, say to yourself, "Be." Hold it a second, then, as you exhale slowly, say to yourself, "Still." Repeat this five times and see if you don't feel more centered and aware of what's going on around you instead of being focused solely on your own thoughts.

When we were young children, we lived "in the moment." We had not yet developed what yogis call the mind of a "drunken monkey"—a mind that lurches from past to future but is never able to stay focused on the present. Often our ability to stay focused starts to disappear when we leave childhood and enter puberty. A prayer poem I wrote for Julia when she was twelve mourns the loss of innocence and joy that accompanied her ability to live in the moment as she did when she was a young child.

Today I Woke Up Empty

My soul completely flown
As if my Self had lost its way
My song had lost its tone.
Today I woke up numbed inside
My feelings paralyzed
As if my mind had given up
The light inside my eyes.

Today I woke no little girl
But someone not yet here
As if I'd lost the faith to grow
In God instead of fear.

PRAYERS ON MY PILLOW

As grown-ups, most of us have lost our faith to "grow in God instead of fear." We no longer hear the clear and joyous voice of spirit that kept us grounded in the here and now. Tibetan Buddhist masters teach that little children are with the Tao, or in the present, naturally in balance with nature and at peace with self.

"I remember once when I was a real little kid walking down the beach all by myself. I didn't have to worry about getting lost, because it was a straight line, and I didn't have to worry about drowning, because I was on the sand. It was such a perfect day. I will never forget how happy I was."

Justine, age 20

"I was seven, and my dad and I were rolling around on the floor, playing and tickling, and my mom was there watching and laughing."

Sue Ann, age 32

"Maybe I was six. I was fishing with my older brother off Newport Pier on a hot day. I just remember thinking how I never wanted that time to end."

Rickie, age 45

"My most spiritual moment when I was very young was one time camping with my family in the Sierra Mountains. They let me sleep outside the RV under the stars, and there must have been a meteor shower or something that night, because I stayed awake all night watching shooting stars."

Sara, age 16

"I have had a really hard life and have fought in my head for years for one happy memory, but have yet to remember one that did not have something bad attached to it. I live now for happy moments for my children and myself."

Nancy, age 33, mother of two girls, ages 12 and 15

"Hearing my grandfather preach in his church one Easter Sunday with the light coming in through the stained-glass windows behind him."

Shantell, age 18

"I remember playing a game with everyone in my family seated around the table. Or maybe it was a puzzlc. I was the youngest and so proud that they'd let me play."

Gloria, age 21

What was one perfect moment that you remember from childhood?

I REMEMBER A MOMENT OF BEING AWARE OF THE MYSTERY AND BEAUTY OF LIFE WHEN I WAS . . .

After we are grown, being in the moment does not come naturally but instead seems to require concentration and practice. We must relearn what it is to be a child. This means allowing ourselves to be more open and trusting of what our heart tells us.

Connecting in the moment changes, well, from moment to moment. If we are trying to connect with another person, we are asking ourselves to see that person exactly as they are now, and to respect them for their unique presence. What do we gain from this effort? Balance. Integration. Love. Wonder. As Charlotte Joko Beck describes in her book *Nothing Special: Living Zen*: "Living is about wonder. As you go through your day, through your little upsets and difficulties, ask yourself, 'Where is the wonder?' It's always there. Wonder is the nature of life itself. We can't force ourselves to feel it. We can only work with the barrier we are facing. The barrier is created by ourselves."

Teachers and authors from many different faiths agree that you have to be utterly in the present to find the wonder and magic in life. No matter where we are, what we are doing, or how we feel, the more we are in the moment, the more we experience the wonder of life.

"I have just about stopped taking photographs of events in my daughter's life because I finally realized that, in capturing these 'Kodak moments,' I wasn't sharing in them."

Candice, age 41, mother of fifteen-year-old

We are not searching for "Kodak moments" here. We are strengthening our natural ability to experience the extraordinary in the ordinary details of every day. There is nothing we can do to make these "moments of being" happen except shift our awareness to what is real. There's no formula except to gently bring our mind back to the here and now. There is no outcome except that we can then appreciate the wonder of everything around us, including our daughters.

Describe for your daughter a recent moment when you were fully and clearly perceptive of what was going on around you—a simple moment when you experienced the wonder of life. It could be anything from drinking a glass of water to walking to the car. For, in the words of Charlotte Joko Beck, it is "nothing special."

A RECENT MOMENT OF WONDER . . .

If we are able to give full attention to even a few moments each day and realize the wonder of what is going on around us, and then share that wonder with our daughters, our relationship deepens. Moreover, if our relationship is on shaky ground, as all mother-daughter relationships are at times, building on the most ordinary of moments, step by step, little by little, enables us to reconnect. When we connect in the moment, we say to our daughters, "I love you *right now* for what you *are*."

I love Emily for being clear on the difference between right and wrong and being able to stand up for her convictions. I also love her for other qualities associated with her certitude, such as stubbornness and a certain defensiveness (as in, "What do you mean I'm not using my time wisely? I *always* use my time wisely."). Like me, if you are connecting with your daughter in the moment, you love her both ways:

I LOVE YOU FOR WHAT YOU ARE . . .

I LOVE YOU FOR WHAT YOU ARE THAT IS NOT
NECESSARILY WHAT I WOULD HAVE CHOSEN FOR YOU
TO BE . . .

I associate sewing with the times when my mother, Patricia, and I were "in the moment together." My mother used
to make most of my clothes: dresses, jumpers, and Hal-
loween costumes when I was little, and then, when I was
older, through my college years, dresses, skirts, slacks, and
prom dresses. My mother remembers our sewing moments
like this:

> I never had a sewing lesson in my life. I just started
> sewing for you when you were a baby. I recollect
> making you two ruffled organdy pinafores when

you were two or so, one in white and one in yellow, that you would have worn to bed if I had let you. Later on I'd sew matching holiday dresses for you and your little sister, same style, different color. But it was in high school that we really got into the business. We'd buy the materials and patterns together and I'd go to work. I got so I could do an item in a day; slacks, skirt, blouse. Villager clothes were all the rage, so we'd pick out a sweater, and then we'd get matching material for the A-line skirt that went with it in the stores. Remember that formal I once made in just one day? We went to Danneman's and picked out velvet in a wine color and put it with some gorgeous silk organza in pink with embroidered wine roses on it that I'd bought years before, and I sewed you into the dress that night minutes before you were picked up by your date for the dance.

These were times when we put aside our differences and related as equals. When we picked out a dress pattern from the pattern books (Butterick patterns were easier to make, but Vogue patterns were far more stylish, so we'd go back and forth), material, and trimming, both of us were focused and thoughtful, aware of each other's special qualities that were making this sewing project possible. Later, when I would try the garment on, first inside out, with the pieces straight-pinned together, then after the seams had been sewn, and then later still, for a final fitting and hemming, we worked as a team. I would stand in front of a mirror, turning slowly, with my mother stooped down beside me, her mouth full of pins, marking the hem. We would discuss when I would wear the garment, how it had turned out, and, of course, debate the length.

"I remember going to the library this one time with my mom when I was real little. I can even remember how it smelled. We checked out a bunch of books for her to read to me."

Susan, age 40

"Once when I was very little I found a turtle in the backyard, and I was so afraid my mother wouldn't let me keep it, but she did. She even helped me make a little house for him. It was the happiest moment when she said yes, you can keep it."

Esther, age 15

"My mama used to braid my hair. There was this one time before my birthday when she wouldn't let me look in the mirror until she was done. When I saw myself, I loved her so much for making me pretty."

Alysa, age 16

"I grew up on a farm. One spring night, I must have been around four, my mother took me with her out to the barn, where one of our dairy cows was dropping her calf. She asked me to help her do something, I don't remember what. But I'll never forget walking back to the house afterward with all the stars out, and she was holding my hand, and I thought I was so grown up."

Chelsea, age 35

"My mom and I found this lost dog, and we went all around the neighborhood until we found its owners. And I was late to school and she was late for work, but we didn't care."

Danielle, age 10

"One time my stepmother and I both picked the exact same dress for me to wear to a dance even though we weren't shopping together. When we both pulled the dresses out to show each other, we were both, like, 'This is bizarre.' I remember thinking, Boy, we're more alike than I thought."

Ashley, age 18

Many of us have literally spent years trying to alter our personas in order to please others. After we become mothers, we try to be whatever we think a mother should be, so it is difficult for us to stop and simply *be*. Spiritual parenting experts repeatedly tell us to celebrate the wonder of our children and our ability to mother them *now*. They say we will only experience needless frustration if we worry about whether or not we're being good parents, or if our children, when grown, "will turn out all right."

It is sometimes hard not to approach mothering as if we were baking a soufflé, worrying the whole time about whether it will rise or fall. Yet why not reap the rewards of being a good mother to your daughter now rather than later? To receive that reward, we must:

1. *Be patient* and *open to however the reward reveals itself.*

2. *Be aware of* yourself *in the moment. Ask yourself,
   "What reward did I receive today for being myself to
   my daughter?"*
3. *Wait, in stillness, keeping your mind present and ob-
   servant. See if you can experience an answer.*
4. *Write down for your daughter* whatever *comes into
   your mind:*

MY REWARD FOR BEING MYSELF WITH YOU IS . . .

If we can stop ourselves from making judgments about
our daughters and simply experience them as who they are
now, we connect in the moment. However, when we are not
mindful and are, instead, *mindless*, we cannot take advantage
of the invitations our daughters give us to be in the moment
with them. These invitations are not always offered with

words. They can also be communicated with silence, body language, tone of voice, or facial expression.

Often our responses are formulaic, even though we recognize the invitation. We want to connect; we even *think* we are connecting, but in reality, we do not stick around, at least mentally, to actually *experience* the connection. We are physically in conversation with them, but we are also someplace else, either in the past or in the future.

Here are things I still say that show I am not present with my daughter: "That's nice." "Tell me later." "It's not that big a deal." "Well, just as long as you had a good time." "Don't think about it." "Not now." "Save it." What do you say when you are not listening to your daughter?

OKAY, I ADMIT IT, SOMETIMES WHEN YOU'RE TRYING TO TELL ME SOMETHING, I SAY . . .

Another way I lose an opportunity to be in the moment with my daughter is when I fill in a pause with a statement indicating I'm concerned not with the present, but with the future, like: "So what are we going to do about:

1. *your grades?"*
2. *your clothes?"*
3. *your attitude?"*
4. *your room?"*
5. *your friends?"*

"I know it's a long way off, but have you thought about:

1. *when you plan to do your summer reading?"*
2. *where you want to go for your birthday?"*
3. *how you are going to study for finals?"*
4. *who you're going to invite to the dance?"*
5. *what you'd like for dinner?"*

Have you ever filled a pause with blather just because you were uncomfortable with the silence? We would be surprised how often our girls are perfectly happy sharing silence.

THERE ARE TIMES WHEN I TALK ABOUT STUFF TO
FILL UP A SILENCE, LIKE WHEN I SAY TO YOU . . .

There are days when Emily looks at me as if I am out of my
mind because for the third or fourth time I will have asked
her, "How are you getting home tonight?" and she will have
patiently told me each time. Have you ever repeated a question that you've asked and your daughter has answered?

I MUST HAVE ASKED YOU . . .

AND EACH TIME YOU SAID . . .

"My mom assumes she knows every detail about me. She thinks she knows me like a book, when in reality she has no clue. She tries to analyze a situation for me, or throws something in my face because she thinks she has it all figured out."

Crystal, age 17

"I don't like the fact that she makes it so hard for me to open up to her. She holds me at arm's length."

Kim, age 14

"I'm afraid to let her into my heart without her taking advantage of it and betraying me."

Jasmine, age 12

"Around my mom I can't be myself because I am supposed to be perfect when I am not. Also I can't talk about my depression. I don't know how to tell my mom I need help. I am actually scared. Enough. I am crying now."

Lisa, age 13

"It's like she thinks that I can't take care of myself, or like I won't take responsibility for my own actions. And when I try to talk to her, it's like she can't just sit still and listen. She always has to nod her head and say, 'Well, maybe you shouldn't have done that, you know?' "

Holly, age 16

"She either asks too many questions or completely ignores me, but either way I don't feel like she wants to be around me anymore. That hurts my heart."

Gillian, age 16

"I'd love to have more time with her . . . I want to share with her some parts of my life, not always just be commenting on what I see her doing without me."

mother, age 44, of thirteen-year old

"I'd like for us to be friends that tell each other almost everything. Right now the only time I feel like that is happening is when we stand side by side in church so we can sing together and bounce to the beat of the music."

Lanie, age 49, mother of sixteen-year-old

"I don't want to cramp her style, but I want to be a part of her life. I just don't know how to go about it."
Darlene, age 32, mother of twelve-year-old

"I try to be there for her, but not be too nosy. I know I ask too many questions, but I can't help myself."
Joannie, age 30, mother of eleven-year-old

"I am often too busy or too tired to pay much attention to her."
Sally, age 38, mother of ten-year-old

Spiritual parenting experts point out that every child is perfect. We can experience what is unique and wonderful about them only if we are less concerned about the kind of job we're doing as mothers.

You may be saying to yourself, *Well, if I'm myself instead of a "mother," who knows what kind of a person I'll be? I may be who I am, and then what will happen?* Our daughters are more understanding than we think. They want us to be real.

"The time I felt closest to my mom was one time when she got really upset about something and started to cry. At first I was scared, but then I was happy that she could cry in front of me."

Shirley, age 13

"One time I was helping my mother cook dinner for my grandparents and she dropped the chicken on the floor, and she said, 'Oh shit,' and that surprised me that she said that, and then we decided to put it back on the plate and not tell anyone. I'll never forget it."

Laurel, age 10

"I love my mama best when we are laughing together."

Shontelle, age 9

"The biggest problem I have with my mother is I can't be myself."

Ryan, age 15

"When I am with my mom we are both pretending to be people we're not."

Crystal, age 14

"I don't know what you mean by this question: 'Do you let your daughter see your true self?' I'm her mother, so that would not be appropriate."

Angela, age 44

"The best thing I can do for my girls is to show them that it's okay to be human."

Portia, age 50, mother of two teenage girls

What is something about you as "you," not as a "mother," that you have been reluctant to tell your daughter?

I AM REALLY QUITE . . .

What do you think your daughter would appreciate knowing about your humanness that you have not shared with her, but always meant to?

I THINK THAT YOU WOULD LIKE TO KNOW THAT . . .

Each Moment of the Day

Can be a miracle,
For beauty shines
If I look with truthful eyes
And love grows
If I give with a generous soul.
Each minute of the day
Can be a miracle,
For wisdom builds
If I learn with an open mind
And joy comes
If I live with love in my heart.

MORE PRAYERS ON MY PILLOW

May every act I take be done with love

Then I will grow strong from within

To make my choices based on truth

The more I see, the more I hear

The more I love, the more I care

THREE

Connecting with Story

Stories Can Be Stated, Shouted, or Sung

Drummed and doodled or danced until done,
Whispered, whimpered, waved like a flag,
Pleaded, promised, put in a bag,
Chanted, chosen, chewed on like gum,
Looked at, laughed at, told on the run.

Stories can be written, wrapped up, and sent,
Crayoned, chalked, or collected like rent,
Folded, faxed, found hidden in halls,
Painted, plastered, pinned up on walls,
Sculpted, scripted, scrambled when told.
There's never a way a story can get old.

PRAYERS ON MY PILLOW

"All my life through stories, those I read, and those I write, I have been building a theology. The term 'theology' means the word about God, and the word about God can be built up of many simple things; it doesn't need to be pompous or pretentious; it is a way of looking at life and asking questions and finding stories. Perhaps we may be asked why we are looking for God in simple stories rather than in learned volumes of theology. And the answer is a story: Once there was a very wise rabbi. A young student came to see him and said, 'Rabbi, in the old days, there were those who saw God. Why doesn't anybody see God nowadays?' And the Rabbi replied, 'Oh, my child, nowadays nobody can stoop so low.'"

TRAILING CLOUDS OF GLORY:
SPIRITUAL VALUES IN CHILDREN'S BOOKS,
BY MADELEINE L'ENGLE

"I love to listen to my mom's stories of when she was growing up. It makes me feel closer to her."

Georgia, age 14

"Before I go to bed my mother makes me tell her a little story. It doesn't have to be a long story. It just has to be a story about something good that happened to me that day, like at school or something."

Toya, age 11

"My grandmother was Sioux. I remember her telling me stories that were really long poems. They were about the people of her tribe and how they lived. Lots of them were about how things came to be and about how you had to always be on the look-out for the spirit world. She was told them by her mother, who was told them by her mother and so on. Those stories are a part of me. They make me who I am."

Renata, age 54

"I was raised on the stories of the saints. My mother was an ardent Catholic and she would read to us about the lives of Saint Teresa and Saint Catherine, a different saint every Sunday. All six of us kids could still tell you pretty much anything you want to know about the saints."

Mary, age 47

"I like stories that are really intense. If I am into a book, I don't want to eat or sleep or anything. I just want to read. Like that's what I did with all the Harry Potter books."

Hallie, age 10

"My favorite kind of stories are true ones."

Brooks, age 15

"I'm living the story of my life every day. But I'm not sure I'll ever find a guy who wants to read it."

Kelly, age 21

"I don't care if a story is true or not, but it's gotta be real. I think it's hypocritical when kids' books turn out all rosy and right when it's never like that in real life."

'Becca, age 13

"When I was a child, I loved hearing stories about my ancestors. The stories were clues about who I was and where I came from."

Joan, age 43

$\mathcal{W}$e all have a need to tell stories—*our* stories. It is in our bones—as much a part of who we are as whether we are fair-skinned or have brown eyes. Telling stories and *reading* stories can be both connective and spiritual. In the Catholic faith there is a special kind of spiritual reading called *Lectio Divina*. In *Lectio Divina* you read with an open heart. You become so intimate and involved in the words that the story becomes a sacred text. When we read with an open heart we allow ourselves to *feel* what we read so that the text takes on a power of its own; the story connects with our soul in ways that nourish and strengthen us.

As parents, we often stop connecting through story. Once our daughters say they are too old for bedtime stories, or cut us off midsentence in a personal reminiscence with an abrupt, "You've told me that story before," we stop. We stop with that particular story, and we stop telling stories or reading them out loud or even listening to them together.

I stopped reading bedtime stories to Emily one night when we were finishing Gary Paulsen's novel *Hatchet*, a tale of survival and a boy's coming-of-age. Emily, who was indulging me, was perfectly capable of reading *Hatchet* to herself and *was* reading it to herself after I left the room. However, I was lingering over every word, acting out every sentence, knowing that this *connection* we had of reading stories aloud, a connection that started with *Goodnight Moon* and *Pat the Bunny*, had become tenuous and was requiring more and more enthusiasm on my part. As I sat on her bed, positively brimming over with anticipation "to find out what happens next," Emily simply said, "Mom, I finished it. He gets rescued." And that was that.

When you *first* started reading stories to your daughter, what was her favorite story?

YOUR FAVORITE STORY WHEN YOU WERE LITTLE WAS . . .

When Emily was around two, her favorite book was *The Puppy Who Had No Home*—a particularly poignant story, as you may have guessed from the title. Her favorite part was this phrase that we would chant together: "Go away little stray, go away I say. And the poor puppy would go away." What was a favorite part of one of your daughter's favorite stories?

YOUR FAVORITE PART OF . . .

Where were you when you read these stories to her? Was she snuggled up in bed? On your lap in a rocking chair? Were you both seated on the floor together?

WHEN WE READ TOGETHER WE WERE . . .

When I was little, my mother read me bedtime stories every night. Two of my favorites were *Raggedy Ann in Cookie Land*, which I must have liked, now that I think about it, because of the story's appallingly sugary setting, and Dr. Seuss's *If I Ran the Zoo*. What was your favorite story as a little girl? Who read to you?

MY FAVORITE STORY WHEN I WAS A LITTLE GIRL
WAS . . .

When did you stop reading bedtime stories to your daughter? Was there a specific time or book, or did the ritual simply trail off? Do you think she remembers?

THE LAST BOOK WE READ TOGETHER WAS . . .

THE REASON WAS . . .

Even after we have stopped reading aloud to our daughters, we can still point them toward stories that strike a chord with them as much as those first bedtime stories did. These are not spiritual stories per se, but stories that, if given a "spiritual reading," will help them successfully navigate life's journey. In Madeleine L'Engle's anthology *Trailing Clouds of Glory,* her choice of books such as *Little Women, Emily of New Moon, Winnie-the-Pooh, To Kill a Mockingbird,* and *Julie of the Wolves* is based on her premise that: "Only as we keep in touch with the child within our very grown-up body can we keep open enough to recognize God who is Love itself, as that Love is revealed in story."

Stories about spiritual values, such as honesty, self-respect, responsibility, courage, and faith, connect us spiritually, no matter what our age, to ourselves, to each other, and to God. When we share a story we become children again. The words of the story become points of light drawing us and our girls together out of the darkness.

"*Charlotte's Web* is still one of my favorite books even though it's very sad when Charlotte dies. I like it because it's honest about death, but also about how life goes on, like at the end when some of Charlotte's babies stay in the barn with Wilbur."

Alicia, age 13

"My fourteen-year-old daughter was trying to get her younger brother to read *The Best Christmas Pageant Ever* for his book report. She was saying something like, 'This is a cool book about a bunch of totally bad kids who don't know anything about Christmas, but then they have to put on a Christmas pageant, so they do it, like, in their own way, which is really dumb, and by the end they find out what God's love is all about.' "

Gail, age 44, mother of three

"My favorite character from a book is Eeyore from *Winnie-the-Pooh*, because he's always having bad days just like me. When my mom says 'Good morning' to me all nice and smiley, I want to answer her like Eeyore: 'Good morning, if it is a good morning, which I doubt.' "

Ingrid, age 12

"When I get homesick, I think about my mother reading me *The Runaway Bunny*, and I feel better. She'll always be there for me, just like the mommy bunny."

Carol Ann, age 19, college freshman

What do you think would be your daughter's equivalent of *The Runaway Bunny* when she's grown and gone? And why?

YOUR *RUNAWAY BUNNY* BOOK MIGHT BE . . .

A publisher of young-adult books says that since preteens and teens do not know what stories to read, they skip all the young-adult stories that might help them in their attempts to make meaning out of life and move on to adult titles. One way to maintain spiritual connections with our daughters through story is to find young-adult books that are about the same themes we held dear as children, and to read them—not out loud together, but separately at the same time, so we can talk about them later. From this concept came Shireen Dodson and Teresa Barker's book on how mothers and daughters could connect through story, *The Mother-Daughter Book Club*. Mothers and daughters meet once a month to experience stories *together*, not only for learning and entertainment, but also as a way to heal relationships.

Our selections will be met with enthusiasm if they are *authentic* and *intense*.

"*The Legacy of Luna* is the most powerful book I have ever read. It's about Julie Butterfly Hill, who lived in this redwood tree named Luna for two years so the loggers wouldn't cut it down. I would recommend this book because even though it's about nature and God, it's very exciting."

Fiona, age 12

"When my eighth-grader chose *A Separate Peace* for her summer reading, I was so pleased because it had been an important book for me as a kid."

Victoria, age 42

"I would recommend *Slave Day*, by Rob Thomas. It's very good because it makes you think about what happens when people are given the chance to show what they would do if everyone wasn't equal."

Nyla, age 15

"I will never forget reading *Lord of the Flies* when I was her age, and now she's reading it and having the same reactions I did."

Margaret, age 52, mother of Allie, age 13

"*Smack*, but you might have to explain to your mom that it's not just about drugs."

Maggie, age 14

"This year the book I liked reading the most was *Whirligig*. It's pretty intense in the beginning because this kid kills someone. Then, later on, when different characters find Brent's whirligigs, it makes them think about what's important in life."

Francie, age 13

What story touched your heart when you were a teenager because it was authentic and intense?

WHEN I WAS YOUR AGE, THE STORY THAT TOUCHED
MY HEART WAS . . .

IT WAS ABOUT . . .

Our daughters may seem cynical and uncaring at times, but in reality they are searching to know themselves and the meaning of the world around them. If your daughter is troubled or has had troubled times, the reading or telling of stories bearing messages that speak to her heart can be a salvation.

Yet our greatest challenge may not be finding the stories, but finding time for her to read them. For it is only through time spent alone with a story that we can experience it and personalize its meaning for ourselves. Stories invite solitude, a condition experienced all too seldom by us or our daughters. Our daughters' time is taken up with sports, extracurricular activities, homework, community service, television, talking to friends on the phone, e-mailing friends, talking to friends on the phone *while* e-mailing them and occasionally performing household chores. Stories simply disappear off the radar screen for all but the most avid readers.

"I don't have time to read for pleasure."

Ryan, age 15

"There seems to be almost no time for us to have a conversation with each other, unless I'm driving her someplace. And in the evenings when we used to read, she's doing homework."

Robin, age 43, mother of Kit, age 12

"I read the books I have to do book reports on . . . sometimes."

Laura, age 13

"I read two pages and then I'm asleep. So then the next night, I don't remember what I read, so I read the same two pages. Don't ask how long it takes me to get through a book."

Hilary, age 50, mother of five

"My grandmother told me stories, but she died."

Sonya, age 18

"No one in our family reads much. But we do watch television together."

Maria, age 40

"My mother used to tell me these great bedtime stories when I was little, but now she goes to bed before I do. We don't even say good night."

Christie, age 17

"We used to sit around the dining room table, and my husband and I would tell the kids stories about, I don't know, everything, our childhood, wild times in college, whatever. We never eat dinner together anymore. Everyone's too busy."

Carole, age 47, mother of three teenagers

"I read stuff off the Internet, but it's usually not stories."

Morgan, age 12

"I study the Bible, and I'd like to talk about it with my children, but they're not interested."

Lonnie, age 45, mother of three

"What do you mean by stories?"

Jenny, age 11

The less we read, the more difficult reading becomes. E-mail may have increased your daughter's typing skills, but how many well-written passages, rich in description, has she encountered while Instant Messenging friends? If we are to reestablish our connections with story, we need to get her attention, as well as focus our own. This doesn't mean we should insist on reading *War and Peace* together or hold nightly storytelling sessions. It does mean prying ourselves away from other activities, if only for a short while, and not necessarily every day, to reconnect with storytelling, in all of its many forms.

How might you make more time in your life to connect with your daughter through stories?

WE COULD MAKE TIME FOR A STORY IF WE . . .

What form might the story take? Reading aloud? Reading the same article, poem, or book and then talking about it?

I COULD IMAGINE A TIME WHEN YOU AND I MIGHT
SHARE A STORY IF . . .

We also tell stories about ourselves. Different from gossip or friendly conversation, which, of course, we also do, storytelling is personal and reflects our understanding that everyone's experience is different but deserves to be heard. Our perspective on ourselves, one another, and life in general changes. This keeps our stories fresh and authentic. It should be an unspoken rule that no one judge the story or the storyteller, which will be the reason your daughter is willing to join in. Our storytelling becomes a window to the true self of the storyteller. If we can trust each other enough to tell our stories honestly, we find common themes and experiences running through each story, however personal, and we feel less alienated.

"My mother tells me stories about when she was a teen girl and about her childhood and I think, wow, she's telling me this."

Lauren, age 13

"The first time my mother told me that she had had an abortion when she was in college, I was, like, I don't want to hear it. But then, after a few days, I asked her to tell me the whole story. Now I know she made mistakes too."

Elizabeth, age 16

"My mom tells me about what she dreamed and I tell her what I dreamed, and sometimes we try to figure out what the dreams mean."

Janice, age 11

"My mom tells stories about when she was my age and got into lots of trouble at school."

Polly, age 11

"I'm always telling her stories about what I went through at her age, but I never start them, 'When I was your age . . .' "

Beth, age 49

"She tells me all the stupid things she did as a teenager, and lets me learn by her mistakes. She also tells me stories about when I was little, and how she couldn't have gotten through my father's death without me. I love her so much."

Patrice, age 15

"I tell her stories about our family that go back for generations. She's always interested."

Liz, age 43

"If I want to get my mother's attention, all I have to do is tell her a story about me and my friends, like what we did at a sleepover or something."

Lauren, age 10

"Once my stepdad and I got into a big fight and I ran away from home. My mom found me, and I told her how I felt and I cried. And my mom told me a story about how she ran away from home when she was my age. I was so surprised and happy cuz I know now that my mom has problems just like everyone else."

Holly, age 13

Share a story with your daughter about a personal experience that you have never told her before.

HERE'S A STORY YOU HAVEN'T HEARD . . .

Sharing our personal stories with our daughters creates new ways for them to think about themselves and their relationships with others. The process breaks down a girl's often self-imposed isolation and relaxes the rigid standards by which she often judges herself and her friends.

Listening to stories ought to be the easiest possible way of connecting with our daughters. Listening requires no props, no specific location, no creativity, memory, experience, education, or intellect, no additional participants except the speaker, and it costs nothing. However, many of us could improve our listening skills.

Ever pretend to listen? I listen, then respond with "right," "that's nice," "and so then what?" while working at my computer, making dinner, reading the newspaper, cleaning the kitchen, or driving the car. I am not listening. Ever start to listen and then find yourself talking instead? Sometimes simply waiting in silence will allow your daughter the space she needs to tell you her story, in her own time.

Listening without an agenda and with full attention would solve many of the communication barriers we have with our daughters. I am guessing that we could all practice fully attentive listening a little more than we do right now. Even maintaining direct eye contact is not enough if you are not really *hearing* what your daughter is saying. It also helps if we can take in what our girls are saying without judging what we hear as "right" or "wrong."

How do you show your daughter that you are *listening* to what she has to say?

I SHOW YOU I AM LISTENING TO YOU WHEN I . . .

"When my mother listens to me, she makes me feel that I am important because what I'm saying is important."

Hannah, age 14

"I make her tell me how she would solve the problem before jumping in with my own suggestions. That way, she begins to trust her own judgments."

Mary, mother of fifteen-year-old

"I'm not a great listener. I'm always interrupting her to give my opinion. It's a fault."

Susanne, age 39, mother of ten-year-old

"My mom doesn't open up to me often. I understand why. I mean, there is an age difference. But when she's having a hard day, she'll tell me all about it, and I just sit and listen, and I think it helps."

Cynthia, age 16

"I try to listen without saying anything about what she's telling me, because I know I'm lucky that she's telling me this story at all."

Charlotte, age 52, mother of three teenage girls

"She tells me her problems and asks me to give my opinion. I am a good listener, but I'm also honest. Sometimes that gets me into trouble."

Katie, age 16

"My mother is usually too busy to listen to me. When I talk to her, she says she is listening, but she's really not, like she will be reading her mail or something."

Dennie, age 13

"I try to give her my complete attention. That means putting down whatever I'm doing at the time, and listening to what she has to say without interrupting her. So far it has kept our communication going."

Sandra, age 46, mother of Emma, age 13

"My parents want me to listen to everything they say, but they aren't interested in hearing what I have to say."

Barbara, age 16

"I don't have to pretend about how I feel around my mom. Even if we both know she does not agree with me, she will listen."

Claire, age 12

"I would like to talk to my mom more, but she is always so tired."

Ann, age 11

Who listened to you, fully and attentively, when you were growing up? How did it feel?

WHEN I WAS A TEEN, _____ LISTENED TO ME . . .

Listening demonstrates our respect for the speaker. When was a time your daughter listened to you fully and attentively?

YOU LISTENED TO ME WHEN I . . .

Could you and your daughter find more time to listen to each other? Come up with some time when the two of you might be together.

WE COULD FIND A LITTLE MORE TIME TO TALK TOGETHER IF WE . . .

Mimi Doe, Debra Whiting Alexander, and Julie and Dorothy Firman, all mothers and authors who write about parenting, agree that listening is critical to establishing a connection with your child. The more we listen, the more our daughters will open their hearts to us and share their stories, experiences, thoughts, and dreams.

When No One Understands Me

When no one wants to hear,
When no one thinks I should be sad
Or be in pain or fear,
When no one sympathizes,
When no one cares a lot,
About the worries inside my heart
About the things I'm not,
When no one has ten minutes' time,
When no one can advise,
Or help me clarify my life,
When my whole life is lies,
Then out of desperation
I look to you and say,
Do you have time to listen
To just one story today?

MORE PRAYERS ON MY PILLOW

Connecting by Acceptance

May I Be

Patient with my weaknesses
Proud of my strengths
Respectful of my feelings
Trustful of my instincts
Loyal to my beliefs
Gentle with my pain
Encouraging to my hopes
Soothing to my anger
Sensitive to my needs
Loving to my soul.

MORE PRAYERS ON MY PILLOW

$\mathscr{A}$cceptance. . .

"My mother accepts my decisions and lets me be very independent because she knows I will turn to her if I need help."

Janna, age 18

"My mom let me give up ballet but keep on with soccer. She was disappointed because she wanted me to keep dancing, but she still let me choose."

Christie, age 11

"She accepts my friends."

Daniela, age 16

"I try to give her some space to be herself, even if I don't approve of everything she does."

Joan, age 45, mother of sixteen-year-old

"I tell her I will love her no matter what. But sometimes I have to bite my tongue to keep from criticizing her friends."

Carole, age 48, mother of thirteen-year-old

---

*N*onacceptance . . .

"She is always judging me."

Ashley, age 13

"My mother's beyond reach. She nags about every little thing about me that's really not a big deal."

Julie, age 15

"She'll be, like, lecturing me on something I did wrong and out of the blue she will yell at me for something different. By the time she is done, I am being punished for a million things instead of one."

Felicia, age 14

"I lose patience and talk down to her."

Betty, age 42, mother of fourteen-year-old

"I tend to be overly controlling. I am the type of person who want results now. I find myself being sarcastic to her. This mistake I make continually."

Melanie, age 38, mother of twelve-year-old

> "I spent my early years with her yelling a lot. Now I'm afraid she'll forget the good times we had and just remember the bad."
>
> *Hollie, age 50, mother of twenty-year-old*

Until Julia left home for college I could not *accept* that she was, in my words, "messy." I would say, "Your room is a mess." She would respond, "It's not a 'mess.' I know where everything is. Anyhow, it's *my* 'mess,' so leave it alone." This should have been a minor issue. I made sure it was a major issue that plagued the two of us:

One: I nag her on a regular basis about either hanging up her clothes in the closet or putting them in the dirty clothes hamper, making her bed, putting the CDs in their holder, and generally cleaning up her room. This means throwing apple cores, empty soda cans, and scrunched-up wads of paper into the trash can and taking dirty dishes back down to the kitchen.

Two: She says, "Okay," but continues to throw her clothes, clean or dirty, into one large pile in the middle of her bedroom floor, and line up chocolate-milk-filled juice glasses next to her bed.

Three: I become impatient and, while she is at school, put everything away so her room is no longer a "mess," but looks the way I want it to. I feel martyred, yet back in control.

Four: She returns from school to find her "space" has been invaded and, while the room looks tidier, her personal "mess" is gone, including random but important homework assignments and crucial cell phone numbers written on scraps of paper. Moreover, her favorite T-shirts, while now clean, have shrunk. Angry, she calls me "a neatness freak who is obsessed with throwing things away." I tell her she's overreacting. We end by repeating the lines "Your room is a mess" and "It's not a 'mess.' I know where everything is. Anyhow, it's *my* 'mess,' so leave it alone."

Five: I feel guilty, because I am "a neatness freak." For instance, I cannot imagine sitting down at the computer if dishes are unwashed, beds unmade, laundry undone . . . and so on. Sure, I have stacks of papers on the floor of my basement office, but they are very neat stacks. I have been known to rearrange the trash. So, why couldn't I just accept the fact that my personal tolerance for "mess" was different from my daughter's without judging the difference? Julia was not demanding to pierce her lips. She was not doing drugs or failing out of school. She did not have an ex-con boyfriend with a full-body tattoo. All she was asking was that I accept this effort to become her own person.

To find that elusive common ground with our teenage daughters, we must accept who they are, and not who we think or wish they could be. We believe we want the best for them, yet at the same time we are reluctant to admit that what is best may not coincide with what we had in mind.

Often our biases still blind us to what is really going on in our daughter's experience of life. Instead, we focus on judging her behavior as either good or bad, according to our standards. We may not take into consideration her need to separate from us as she tests her independence and develops her own sense of self.

How do you show your daughter that you accept who she is?

I SHOW I ACCEPT YOU BY . . .

How often do we ignore the beautiful presence of our daughters and focus on their petty annoyances? How often do we refuse to give up control over their lives by declaring the following to be *unacceptable*:

Staying up past bedtime, staying up until dawn, eating pizza for dinner six nights in a row, talking on the phone, forgetting where the phone is, wearing too much makeup, wearing too skimpy a tank top, and waiting until the last minute to: study, make social plans, shower, fill in the SAT application, fill in any application, tell us that it is their turn to provide the team or cast breakfast, get directions, RSVP, or buy their friend's birthday present.

When were you so engaged in your daughter's life that you could not accept something petty and insignificant that she did?

I ADMIT IT. I COULDN'T HELP MYSELF WHEN I MADE A BIG DEAL OUT OF YOUR . . .

This does not mean we accept behavior that is life-threatening, unhealthy, unethical, or unwise. However, to connect through acceptance, we might be a little more tolerant of our daughter's need to stretch, to take risks, to come up against her own weaknesses, and to discover her own strengths—for herself. We might be a little more choosy about choosing our battles.

Recall a recent time when you judged your daughter's behavior to be unacceptable, but let it go?

I DID NOT APPROVE, BUT I ACCEPTED IT WHEN YOU . . .

As Ann Tremaine Linthorst says in her book *Mothering as a Spiritual Journey*: "The belief that puberty is a kind of magic wand that turns otherwise delightful children into a crazed and alien species is another one of those idiotic human beliefs that must be consistently refused admission into consciousness." Other parenting experts agree that when we face separation from our daughters because they are growing up, we worry that we will lose our control over them and their love for us.

"I am so afraid that my daughter will fall prey to the wrong crowd . . . the bad influences and end up being hurt no matter what I do to prevent it."

> *Tamera, age 50, mother of fourteen-year-old*

"I fear that she will fall away and make all the stupid mistakes I did. I want to break the cycle for her, so she'll have it better."

> *Carol Ann, age 46, mother of sixteen-year-old*

"I worry that my girls will get in with the wrong people and get into drugs and drinking."

> *Verlina, age 42, mother of two teenage girls*

"My biggest fear is that I will repeat the mistakes my mother made and she will hate me."

> *Amy, age 38, mother of eleven-year-old*

"She will judge me and find me a bad mother."

> *Ellyn, age 51, mother of seventeen-year-old*

"I will fail as a mother."

> *Helen, age 43, mother of twelve-year-old*

"What if I can't stop the pain and hurt that my daughters must suffer just to grow up?"

Renae, age 40, mother of two middle-school girls

"I fear that she will forget the values I have tried to teach her and will end up drinking and having sex at an early age because of the crowd she hangs out with."

Joanie, age 42, mother of fifteen-year-old

What do you fear for your daughter now that she is growing up?

MY FEAR FOR YOU IS THAT . . .

Acceptance requires *understanding* that this person is experiencing her life, not yours. Acceptance means *trusting* that there is an essential goodness within her, and within you. Acceptance demands you to *respect* her ability to cope with her fears.

Understanding
Trusting
Respecting

The challenge for you now is to make the leap from fear to trust. In so doing, you say that you understand her need to separate her life from yours.

I TRUST THAT YOU WILL . . .

"I tell my mom that I can be trusted from past experiences and she should know I can handle the responsibilities of being independent."

Sara, age 14

"Mom, I'm not a little child anymore. I can make respectful decisions and think about it long and carefully."

Rashawn, age 16

"I quote her: 'Sometimes you have to learn the hard way, and make mistakes.' "

Brittany, age 13

"I haven't screwed up majorly in the past, and I'm very responsible."

Crystal, age 16

"I may make the same mistakes you did, but I want them to be on me. I want to experience these problems myself."

Kelly, age 15

"I've never done anything to make you not trust me, yet you do not let me do anything. You are too closed-minded."

Carmine, age 13

"Mom, I know you love me and are scared, but you need to let me live. Let me go."

Melissa, age 17

"Don't compare me to my sister or my friends. Accept me for me."

Jennifer, age 13

"If you paid as much attention to what I do right as you do to what I do wrong, you'd let me do more things."

Georgia, age 12

Think about a time when your daughter says to you, "Accept me?

I AM LISTENING TO YOU WHEN YOU SAY . . .

Remember when you were a teenager and were asking for your independence? Remember demanding more "space" from your mother?

I USED TO TRY TO CONVINCE MY MOTHER TO ACCEPT MY BEHAVIOR BY SAYING . . .

While our daughters may be changing on the *outside*, inside, their inner selves remain the same as when they were little girls. Seeing that inner self is easier if we look for those values or qualities that we delighted in when our daughters were little children. Rediscover her affectionate nature, playfulness, honesty, grace, generosity, and courage. See her for what she is by looking below the surface to her heart.

Showing your child that you see the love and innate goodness in her heart will help *her* see those qualities as well. Many teens are convinced they are disappointments to their parents, and have "let them down." They set the bar so high for themselves that they have a difficult time accepting their own frailties and mistakes as a natural part of growing up.

What is a wonderful quality of your daughter, a part of her inner spirit that remains constant as she changes from child to adolescent?

YOU HAVE ALWAYS POSSESSED THE MOST WONDERFUL QUALITY OF . . .

It is honest, and even spiritual, to admit to ourselves that there are times when our daughters are not people we like—to talk to, look at, or be with. There are plenty of times when neither I nor my daughters are at our best, and that ought not to harm our relationship. When I am confronted with a sullen, withdrawn fourteen-year-old who answers in monosyllables if at all, my first reaction is not, "How adorable she is today. What a blessing." On the other hand, I must look for some way to tell this angry young person that she is as loved as when she was six years old and cuddling up next to me in my bed.

We want to avoid demanding a relationship in which the two of us are only acceptable to each other when we are both on our best behavior. The false self we then maintain in order to please is not the inner self or soul who yearns to be accepted unconditionally.

Our loving acceptance becomes even more critical because this is the time when peer relationships can be cruelly judgmental and difficult to maintain with integrity. Although she had many girlfriends all through secondary school, Julia never found a friend she could "be herself with" until she went to college. So I wrote this for her:

I Need a Friend to Talk To

To share my hopes and fears.
I need a friend to be with
To share my jokes and tears.
I need a friend to give me
The honesty I seek
To listen and to offer
Her strength when I feel weak.

I'll give her all my secrets,
Our love will know no bounds.
I'll treat her as a sister,
A partner in life's rounds.
Our talks will be so precious
Yet never really end.
I'll not be truly happy
Until I have this friend.

PRAYERS ON MY PILLOW

Describe for your daughter how you have been her "friend to talk to" recently. If you haven't been, what might you tell her to convince her that you could be?

I AM YOUR MOTHER, BUT I AM ALSO YOUR FRIEND
WHEN . . .

Yet, how do we convince our daughters that we accept
them for who they really are when they doubt our sincerity?

> "My mother tells me I'm pretty, but I don't believe
> her because she's my mother."
>
> *Ellen, age 14*
>
> "She tells me she doesn't care if I get C's, but under-
> neath, I know she cares a lot."
>
> *Sandra, age 12*

"My mother's such a hypocrite. She tells me she trusts me, but then when I go someplace with my friends, she's always suspicious about what we're going to do, like we're going to get into trouble."

Kelly, age 16

"My mom is always saying how we should spend more time together, just hang out, but she's always too busy to actually do it."

Natalie, age 14

"I wish my mother approved of who I am."

Jill, age 16

"I can't convince her that she is beautiful and that this is just an awkward stage she's going through. She says everyone at school thinks that she's ugly and so she must be."

Hilda, age 40, mother of eleven-year-old

"How do you convince your fourteen-year-old that her body is adorable just the way it is, and she's not 'fat'? All her friends are dieting. What do you say?"

Margaret, age 45, mother of fourteen-year-old

We can be *mindful* of how actions speak louder than words. We role model (1) accepting ourselves for who we really are, and (2) trusting our daughters to accept us for who we really are.

Discovering who we are and then accepting ourselves is a lifelong journey.

My journey seemed to have gotten off to a bumpy start. Here is how my mother recalls my friendship with Danny when I was four:

> Danny was very rambunctious. He would come over and jump up and down on our glider swing on the front porch or play in mud and then track it through the house—all sorts of things we didn't want him or anyone else to do. You thought it was marvelous, though, and joined him in whatever he wanted to do and laughed at everything he did. We tried to tell you that you shouldn't go along with another child who was doing wrong and that you could make up your own mind. We were upset and frustrated with you and told you we didn't approve. It was the first time I felt frustrated and unsure of being a parent.

In my defense, we had just moved to the neighborhood and, during that summer, Danny was my *only* friend. But in retrospect I agree: I should not have jumped up and down on the glider just because Danny did.

My need to be accepted continued, peaking in adolescence when I created fictional identities for myself. I firmly believed that others would find the girl I was pretending to be far more acceptable than the girl I really was.

I grew up an "air force brat," and from ages eleven to fifteen I changed schools at least once a year. Each move to a new air base meant adjusting to a new environment and making new friends. I remember myself in seventh grade, standing fearfully outside an English class at a base school on the outskirts of Tokyo, trying to get up the nerve to open the door. I was tall for my age, gangly, with braces on my teeth, eyeglasses, and pimples. I had not a clue about how to act in order to be accepted and liked.

I started reinventing myself. In eighth grade, at another school in Japan, I turned myself into "Sam," the tough girl, an early sixties version of Rizzo in *Grease*. I wore a leather jacket and used to sneak out of the house to ride around Tachikawa Air Force Base on the back of my boyfriend's motorcycle. I was always in trouble and was "grounded"—in today's vernacular—on a regular basis. I was unhappy and confused about who I was. Here is how my mother remembers that time:

> In sixth, seventh, and eighth grades you were going through that clique period that so often girls of that age go through. There was a period of leaving you out of their little secrets and times together and you were devastated. We felt awful because you didn't

want to come to Japan anyway, and now you were miserable. We found out you were hiding in the girls' lavatory at recess rather than be with the other girls. When I heard this, I called and made an appointment to see your home room teacher. But I was so emotionally upset at the problem that when I got in his office, I started to cry and could hardly speak. Eventually things got better and you became part of a group. It was a hard time for you, and for me, too.

It was a hard time for us, but not as hard as the next year, when we moved to Montgomery, Alabama. I entered Bellingrath Junior High as "Toni" from Paris. I spoke with a French accent. I don't remember why I thought I could maintain this persona without actually knowing any French, but I managed to charm both students and faculty for weeks before being found out. Of course, when I had to come clean, I was humiliated.

Did you ever struggle to be accepted when you were your daughter's age?

WHEN I WAS AROUND YOUR AGE, I AND TRIED TO BE
ACCEPTED BY . . .

I have a long way to go before I can fully accept who I
am, but my efforts have been observed and appreciated by
my daughters. How have you shown your daughter that you
are still learning about who you are?

I APPRECIATE THAT YOU KNOW I STRUGGLE WITH
ACCEPTING THIS ABOUT MYSELF . . .

If we can trust our daughters to accept us for who *we* really are, we are automatically on common ground. By revealing our true selves to our daughters, we show them our spirit and our heart. In accepting us for who we are, they will open to our acceptance of them.

"My mom knows she can cry in front of me, and it just makes me think she is stronger."

Hannah, age 15

"She tells me things about when she was a teen girl that I thought she never would, and I'm so glad she does. I love her for it."

Victoria, age 13

"She knows I know how stressed out she gets sometimes about work and my father and that I understand."

Francie, age 16

"I love my mom for all the dumb things she does, because I know she understands when I do something dumb, like once she forgot she had invited people over for dinner and they came."

Lauren, age 10

What about you does your daughter accept unconditionally, perhaps even more than you do yourself?

I LOVE YOU FOR ACCEPTING MY . . .

Be with Me

When I stand
Facing the world
And am judged.
Expressionless
I do not speak
But take responsibility
For my Self.
Be with me then.

MORE PRAYERS ON MY PILLOW

Connecting in Sacred Space

A Place to Find Myself

Sometimes it's hard to find a place
To be alone without disgrace,
A place where I can cry and scream
Or simply close my eyes and dream,
A place where no one comes to see
What I am doing or if I'm free.
Sometimes it's hard to find a spot
To be myself and not be caught,
As though to be alone is bad,
A sign I'm fearful, sick, or sad.
What they don't see and I can't say
Is being alone is my time to pray.

PRAYERS ON MY PILLOW

Sacred space is a place where you can go and feel safe and bring forth what you are and what you might be. At first you might find that nothing happens there. But if you have a sacred place and use it, you will eventually find yourself again and again.

JOSEPH CAMPBELL

"My sacred space is a path in a park near my house where I walk my dog. Nobody else goes there. It is especially pretty in the fall when all the leaves turn red and yellow."

Melanie, age 11

"My special place is the stairs in a Mexican restaurant on Forty-second Street in NYC. It is always extremely crowded and we always eat on the second floor, and because it's such an open restaurant, the smoke from the first floor rises up and makes the stairs all mysterious in a scary Mexican restaurant sort of way. I wish I could spend longer on those stairs."

Rachel, age 12

"My house in Zimbabwe has a wonderful garden and fruit trees and a birdbath. It is my sacred space because it means a lot to me even though I'm not there now."

Oluche, age 14

"My favorite place is the sunroom in my house. It is warm and cozy with a big couch and windows looking out over our backyard. I like to sit there and think."

Marie, age 13

"My sacred space is in my bedroom, where I have all my favorite things on a shelf near my bed like pics of my friends, my journal, my stuffed owl, my incense candle, and my retainer."

Suzy, age 11

I first learned about sacred space from my grandmother Geneal. When I was four years old my family moved to Lafayette, Indiana, so that my father could teach ROTC at Purdue University. We rented an old Victorian house with a wraparound porch, and a backyard that went on forever (or so it seemed to a four-year-old), with a flower garden and an apple orchard. There were few young children my age for me to play with, but I had my stuffed animals and dolls, and life was pretty good that summer until my mother brought home a new baby sister.

Christine came into the world frail and sickly, and to make matters worse, my mother returned home ill herself from a difficult pregnancy and cesarean birth. So her mother, Geneal, flew from New Delhi, where my grandfather was posted by the State Department, to help out. As soon as Grandma arrived, it became obvious to me that the entire household's attention was going to focus on the person in the freshly wallpapered nursery. Young officers' wives invaded the house to wash diapers and sterilize bottles under the imposing command of Geneal who, in India, had a staff of eight and knew how to give orders. I resented them. I resented my bedridden mother, and I *especially* resented my baby sister.

I tried to draw attention back to where it rightfully belonged by being, for the first time in my life, "naughty." I drew on the walls with my crayons. I took scissors to the ruffles on my pink organdy party dress. I "talked back," and I stopped eating. Meals were taken seriously by our family. Everyone was expected to be on time, in place, and demonstrably appreciative of the food by eating everything on their plates. Once my self-imposed fast was determined to be caused by sheer stubbornness and not a stomach flu, mealtime became a torturous battle of wills often ending with me seated at the table alone, defiantly staring at cold, congealed mashed potatoes after everyone else had left.

One morning I wandered into the little den that had been converted into Geneal's bedroom and found her seated, motionless, eyes closed, in front of a table with the most beautiful and exotic collection of objects I had ever seen: a carved box inlaid with coral and turquoise, a polished stone, an ivory statue of a Hindu goddess, a lighted candle—imagine, at ten o'clock in the morning—and burning incense. She must have sensed me, because she opened her eyes, beckoned me closer, and introduced me to the concept of sacred space. She explained that she took these objects with her wherever she went to create a "special place" where she could be alone and quiet and just "herself." And then, seeing how fascinated I was, she suggested we find a similar "special place" just for me.

It took only a day or so for me to inhabit my first of many sacred spaces—an old apple tree with twisted branches so low to the ground that even a little girl could climb up and hide among the leaves. I called it my "jiggley wiggley" tree, and when I showed it to Geneal for approval, she immediately noticed the deep hole in the trunk where she was quite certain fairies lived.

The next day an old bedspread mysteriously appeared, hung over the two lowest branches, providing a safe hiding place where I could play. At Geneal's suggestion I made cunning little "rooms" out of buttons and seashells, rocks and sticks decorated with moss for the fairies to live in when I was asleep. But by far, the most *sacred* time I spent in that particular space was mealtime. Geneal decreed that, for the next month, I was to be allowed to eat one meal a day, my choice, breakfast, lunch, or dinner, in the jiggley wiggley tree by myself, unattended. And, if I wished, I could eat it on doll dishes. Sibling rivalry gave way to utter bliss.

What is the earliest memory you have of creating a space for yourself as a child? Or having someone like my grandmother create it for you?

WHEN I WAS A CHILD, MY SACRED SPACE WAS . . .

Thirty years later I confronted a similar situation when Julia was four years old and I brought home her new baby sister, Emily. I was a little slower on the uptake than Geneal, due, I like to think, to sleep deprivation. However, after a few weeks of Julia's temper tantrums, her new fear of the dark, and her sudden refusal to eat anything but Campbell's chicken noodle soup, I remembered the jiggley wiggley tree. We found the perfect space for her: an empty closet big enough to hold a beanbag chair, some toys, and a cassette player. As Julia grew older, her choice of spaces changed. One summer, it was outside in the backyard in a tree house. Later, it was the lower bunk of her bunk bed pushed into the corner of the bedroom to make it as cozy as possible.

When I talk to mothers and daughters about sacred space, we discuss the differences between places of communal worship such as churches, synagogues, mosques, temples, and shrines. We agree that each faith has a unique perspective on how sacred space ought to look, and how it is used. We also consider the magic and mystery of historic or natural sacred spaces like the pyramids in Egypt, Stonehenge in England, Mount Fuji in Japan, the Ganges River in India, or the temple at Delphi in Greece. We discuss how we can feel peace and connectedness in both the more formal sacred spaces and the special personal places we create for ourselves. We talk about what makes a place of the spirit, and how we, often without realizing it, create sacred space for ourselves. Then everyone describes a place of spirit that they consider their *personal* sacred space.

> "My place of spirit is my kitchen. That's where I cook for my family, I read, I make my jewelry, I drink pots of coffee. Sometimes it is where I pray."
>
> *mother of thirteen-year-old*

> "My bedroom, which I have decorated just the way I want it in my favorite color, green."
>
> *Mary, age 10*

> "My special place is my bedroom. Actually it's my king-sized bed. I love crawling into bed, and snuggling under the quilt. My kids like it, too, but it's not special for them. It's my ship against the storm."
>
> *mother of three, ages 9, 11, and 14*

> "My church. Even though it's not where we live, it's my home and my community."
>
> *mother of seven, ages 6 to 24*

"My grandmother has, like, this little booth in her kitchen just big enough for one person to sit. It's right under a window where her canary lives in his cage. That is my very favorite spot."

Angela, age 9

"My sacred space is definitely my garden. When I'm working in my garden, and that means doing anything from weeding to turning soil to picking flowers, I am at peace."

mother of two, ages 11 and 13

"My sacred space is my freezer."

Linda, age 13

"I hate to admit this, but as a mother of four kids, I think it's my car."

mother of four

How do you describe your personal sacred place?

MY PERSONAL SACRED SPACE IS . . .

What has your daughter chosen as her sacred space?

AT HOME, YOUR SACRED SPACE IS . . .

What does this space reveal about her to you?

YOUR CHOICE OF SPACE TELLS ME THAT . . .

There were plenty of times during Julia's early adolescence when the two of us completely forgot about sacred space. Since we were often communicating *indirectly* during those times, I would write poems that redefined sacred space for us both. I would search for new words that might lead her back to a place we both knew to be a source of comfort. These lines are an example:

Thank you for this silver carpet
Of moonlight
That spreads across my floor
For me to walk on
As I pray.

PRAYERS ON MY PILLOW

I was hoping she would remember that sacred space is a "safe place" where we can find solace and peace. Our "safe place" can be a *three-dimensional* space like a place of worship, our bedroom, or a private spot in our garden, or it can be a *two-dimensional* space like a window view, photograph, or painting of a place that we endow with spiritual qualities.

I have endowed with spiritual qualities a dirt path behind our house at the beach. The path winds through thick scrub oak and blueberry bushes, and then opens up to a view of where the water and sky meet. The family uses it as a shortcut to either the beach or a paved road. For years I've walked and biked the path alone as well as with my daughters in all four seasons and at every hour of the day. I am always aware not of my destination, but of simply being on the path.

The path resonates with memories of change and growth within our family, yet at the same time certain elements have remained constant. These are the light at different times of day, the sounds of the ocean, the seasons, the earth, and the sky. As I walk, I endow the path with these natural qualities of spirit so that I pass through several landscapes at once: natural, emotional, and spiritual.

"My spiritual place is the hospital chapel where I work as a nurse. Sometimes I go there when it's empty and just sit."

mother of seventeen-year-old

"Behind our temple is a little garden with a bench. It's surrounded by bushes and has green grass. Sometimes I sit there after services and think about God."

Sarah, age 11

"My mom's bed is where I always go to make up after we have a fight. I get into her bed and she rubs my back and gives me a head massage and we both get back together again."

Polly, age 14

"The beach where we vacation each year is where I go to be alone. I walk for miles. It is my safe place. I am comforted by the sound of the waves and the salty smell. In many ways I feel closer to God on my beach walks than I do in church."

mother of three teenage girls

"My special place is a bench near the lilac bush in my backyard. It reminds me of when I was little and the house we lived in had lots of lilacs. I wait all year for spring to come so I can sit there under the blooms and smell the lilacs."

mother of nine-year-old

Is there a place where you or your family go that you have endowed with sacred qualities?

A SPECIAL PLACE FOR ME IS . . .

We can also use guided imagery to help us imagine a sacred space. This is a place we can visit when we feel anxious or "stressed out." Girls imagined:

"I am sitting on a rock in the forest next to a little stream. The rock is covered in green moss and there are lots of ferns. There are rays of light coming through the trees. I sit there for hours just looking at the water."

Samantha, age 12

"My special place is a place I remember dreaming about. It was this big house with high windows like a church. I don't remember much more except I remember feeling so happy there. That's what I try to remember most."

Laticia, age 10

"I imagine a room at the top of a beautiful tower covered with rose vines and the room has huge windows and a balcony and if you went up on the balcony, you could see huge mountains like Mount Everest."

Charlotte, age 14

> "There would be a fountain in the middle with a bench and a path that makes a circle like in the bishop's garden."
>
> *Megan, age 11*

If you were making up a sacred space for yourself, what would it look like?

MY IMAGINARY SACRED SPACE IS . . .

In addition to imagining a sacred space, we can remember a special place from our past and then endow it with those qualities that we consider sacred. At age twelve, Julia described one "place" she could still go to because she remembered how perfect life was at that exact moment in time and space. "It is on a sunny late summer afternoon in our garden when I am three. I see myself seated on the brick patio putting baby powder on my new baby doll. I am wearing my favorite white sundress with pink, blue, and yellow satiny ribbons on the front, and there are big pots of flowers around me."

> "It's this one day at the stable where I go to ride. I'd been cleaning stalls and I was tired, so I decided to climb up into the hayloft. I got up there and, like, almost went to sleep. I could see little specks of dust in the light. I'll always remember that day."
>
> *Roxanne, age 18*

> "I remember the Japanese temple I visited in California where everything was gold and red and you could see light through the walls because they were made of rice paper. There were wind chimes, too. There was a little brook outside. I took off my shoes and went inside. It was very peaceful."
>
> *Brianna, age 13*

> "In my mind I go to the same beach in Delaware that I went to as a kid, so it holds a lifetime of memories for me. I remember a place that's deserted, where I used to go in the early morning. I'd just sit looking out at the waves."
>
> *Connie, mother of two*

Sacred space becomes connecting when it is shared by both you and your daughter. The two of you might enjoy a favorite ocean view or stroll through the woods, or sit together on the stone bench at the bottom of your garden. Even better, the space *continues* to connect and shape your inner self every time you visit it. When we share sacred space we are agreeing that it has a centering or balancing function in our daily lives. For, no matter where our sacred space is, it is a *shelter* or safe haven where we can be ourselves *together*.

> "We both like to read on the same sofa in the den. It is in front of a fireplace but also has a big window with a great view of the woods to the side of our house. When we're having a heart-to-heart talk, that's where we always have it."
>
> *mother of thirteen-year-old*

"Our kitchen, which is our favorite room in the house. It's like neutral territory. Even if we are fighting about something, we sort of put it to the side when we are in the kitchen. Maybe it's because we both like to cook."

Tonika, age 16

"There is a mountain range about thirty minutes from our house with several picnic sites where our family has gone since my daughters were born. Just the other day my oldest and I were talking about how a certain mountain path that we like to climb together before cooking hamburgers or whatever will always hold a special place in our hearts. I guess that path is our sacred space."

mother of two girls, ages 12 and 14

"We have this special corner in our backyard that my mom made for us. It has an arbor with a bench underneath and flowers all around it. There is a little fountain and a stone place where we put a statue of an angel."

Liddie, age 10

In order to create a sacred space, we identify and then arrange to our liking the things that hold special meaning for us. Travis Price, a prize-winning architect whose firm, Spirit of Place, Spirit of Design, designs sacred spaces all over the world and teaches others to build them as well, offers some suggestions to get started:

- *Begin by looking at photographs and paintings of ancient sacred places and natural phenomena. Which appeal to you, and why?*
- *Think about the natural objects you would like to use in a sacred space, such as stones, flowers, shells, water, light, sand, sticks, or plants.*
- *Take a few minutes to walk around the house, the yard, the neighborhood park, or nearby woods to identify potential sacred spaces. Think about the elements that appeal to you. What makes the space special? Is it the light, the colors, textures, or shapes of certain objects? Is it a particular tree? A sweet-smelling flower? The sound of water? Or the sound of silence?*
- *Consider what symbols of your faith resonate most with you and how you might bring them into your space.*
- *Determine what it would take to label a shared space as "sacred" for you and your daughter in terms of objects as well as other additions, subtractions, and*

changes to the overall environment. You might want to add some plants, rearrange the furniture, change the lighting, hang wind chimes, or figure out a way to bring the sound of water into the space in order to make it more soulful.

Here are some more suggestions from Travis Price about what to consider:

Objects:

- *To hold—like a stuffed animal, smooth stone, or string of beads*
- *To look at—like a view or painting of a mountain or a flower; a mirror; an arrangement of flowers, pebbles, pottery; or a fountain*
- *To take comfort from—like a quilt, or a deep, soft throw or a pillow*
- *To capture memories—like photographs to remind us of who we are and who is important to us*

Natural elements or things that are symbolic of nature:

- *Earth—like clay pots, rocks, polished stones, glass, baskets, crystals, wood, metal, cloth, flowers, plants, grasses, or herbs*

- *Fire—like fireplaces, candles, stars, moons, or suns*
- *Water—like oceans, streams, ponds, waterfalls, rivers, or silk*
- *Air—like wind chimes, bells, burning incense, or fans*

Combinations and connections:

- *Combine things in numbers that are significant to you, like three polished stones, two photographs, a single statue, four symbols of the seasons.*
- *Connections can symbolize your life's journey from one passage or stage to another. So you may find that connecting forms such as arches, bridges, paths, spirals, and stairs appeal to you.*

What are some objects you and your daughter might put in a sacred space?

OUR SACRED SPACE COULD INCLUDE THE
FOLLOWING . . .

How might you take an already existing space and make
it more sacred for the two of you?

OUR SHARED SACRED SPACE COULD BE . . .

The concept of shared sacred space may be new to everyone in the family, so think about how to introduce it gradually and indirectly.

"Think out loud" about the introspective qualities of a view, photograph, painting, or place you are visiting together without any expectation of a response.

Point out how we can't help but arrange objects that reflect our inner selves, whether in a garden or on a dressing table, bookshelf, coffee table, or kitchen counter.

Discuss a communal space that is already designated by family members as a calming, contemplative place to go.

Together, try to define what it is about the place that gives those who are there "good energy" and feelings of clarity and focus. In order to increase the good energy, there could be a rule that no one can go there "to pick a fight." In other words, the space is "neutral territory."

Help Me Remember That Moment of Happiness

When I was a child
And my world was a garden,
When I picked wild strawberries alone in the sunlight,
When the air stood still
And I walked in grace,
When my heart was dancing and my soul was one
With the beauty around me and the love inside.

PRAYERS ON MY PILLOW

SIX

Connecting through Creativity

When I Sing My Songs

Or write my poems,
A part of my self is revealed
A part of my heartache is healed.
When I play my notes
Or dance my steps,
A part of my feeling is known
A part of my talent is shown.
When I draw my scenes
Or sculpt with clay,
A part of my dream is released
A part of my soul is at peace.

MORE PRAYERS ON MY PILLOW

When true simplicity is gained,
To bow and to bend we shan't be ashamed.
To turn, turn, will be our delight
Till by turning, turning we come round right.

VERSE FROM "SIMPLE GIFTS," A SHAKER SONG

"My girls and I make desserts together . . . cookies, cakes, pies, puddings. We're always experimenting. Sometimes our 'creations' don't turn out, but we don't care. It's the doing of it that counts."

mother of two, ages 9 and 10

"My daughter and I go on an annual scavenger hunt in the fall. We look for unusual vines, nuts, and other items suitable to include on gift packaging, decorative wall hangings, or as part of a gift itself. Our basket is quickly filled up with interesting finds, but the greatest find is the gift of time together."

mother of sixteen-year-old

"We go to one of those paint-it-yourself pottery places. We started going when my daughter was eight, and now she's fourteen, but once or twice a year we still like to go there and paint stuff."

mother of fourteen-year-old

"My daughter has been taking ballet lessons for years. We attend as many dance performances as we can. Not just ballet, but other kinds of dancing as well. We saw *Stomp*. She loved it."

mother of twelve-year-old

"I make, like, these string bracelets and necklaces for myself and my mom. Then she made one for me. We wear them because we love each other."

Nicole, age 10

"She takes me to museums and tells me stories about the paintings."

Allison, age 9

"We collect scallop shells and then come home and decorate them. Some I give away and some my mom punches a hole through, and we use them as napkin rings."

Jenny, age 12

"I made my mother a menorah out of clay. She uses it every year."

Sara, age 9

"My mother reads her poetry to me over the phone or she e-mails it."

Anna, age 18

We are all artists. Whether we are creating art ourselves, or opening our hearts to the grace and mystery of a beautiful creation by someone else, we are going *beyond the ordinary* in our lives to another level, the level of spirit. Our spiritual self hungers for what is beautiful in the world. When we create or contemplate beauty, our emotions are stirred. We may feel great pleasure or deep pain. We may be in awe at the sheer magnitude and beauty of the creation before us. Gazing up at the ceiling of the Sistine Chapel, we are in awe of the genius of Michelangelo's work. Seeing the Grand Tetons in Wyoming, we are in awe of Nature's work.

We often pass right by opportunities to appreciate the beauty all around us. We are too busy, too scheduled, and, if we stop at all, we are too tired.

Creativity forces us to slow down and look for beauty with our hearts, not our heads. When we look with our hearts, we find beauty in all sorts of things that aren't just "pretty" or perfect. If we include what is unique, individual, and imaginative, we find far more opportunities to appreciate how creativity fills our lives.

Describe in words or in a sketch, something beautiful in your life that is not just "pretty," but which affects you emotionally.

I SEE THE BEAUTY IN LIFE WHEN I LOOK AT . . .

Being aware, every day, of what is original and beautiful keeps us open to what is original and beautiful in ourselves and our daughters.

"I saw the most beautiful flowers today up at the park where I walk my dog. I think they were tulips."

Kristen, age 9

"The most beautiful thing I saw today was my cat. She was in my windowsill."

Becky, age 10

"I would choose the mountains around my house as the most beautiful thing I see every day because when I wake up, I can see them from my bedroom window. They look different depending on the season, but they are always beautiful."

Connie, age 15

"My mother is a potter and she made a great pot today."

Heather, age 14

"My two children asleep on the sofa at midnight before I woke them up to go to bed. That was the most creative, beautiful sight I saw today."

Fran, age 42

"I looked out the window and saw the pair of cardinals who nest each year in the tree outside my kitchen. It was early morning, and I was struck by their beauty. No one can create as well as nature."

Linda, age 39

"The best example of creativity I ran across today was at the drugstore. One of the clerks was rearranging a display of hair products. She was adding little random touches like hair ribbons and clips. When she saw I was watching, she said, 'Might as well make it look good, right?' "

Wendy, age 51

What thing or person made you appreciate the creativity and beauty in everyday life?

TODAY I WAS STRUCK BY THE BEAUTY OF . . .

The gulf between appreciating creativity and being creative isn't as great as you might think. We may be creating art as painters, musicians, actors, poets, scientists, film directors, or architects, but more often than not, we're creating with the materials at hand in the moments that make up our lives. We are creating as mothers, daughters, wives, workers, car poolers, homemakers, or volunteers. For most of us, creative life is made up of the commonplace, from a well-cooked dinner to a well-told bedtime story . . . from painting a ten-year-old's room to taking her to an art exhibit.

What is something you created during the day's activities? It can be anything that takes you beyond the ordinary in your life, past the humdrum and routine to another level of feeling and focus. It can be as spontaneous as lighting candles for a dinner of chicken takeout or pretending to be Diana Ross and dancing around the kitchen lip-synching "Stop! In the Name of Love."

I CREATED SOMETHING BEYOND THE ORDINARY AND
ROUTINE IN MY LIFE WHEN I . . .

Whether we're creating something ourselves or being
moved by someone else's creation, we are going beyond the
ordinary and opening to possibilities of new patterns of thinking, and new *honest* ways of expression.

"Sometimes the poems I write are very angry, but
that's how I feel."

Jillian, age 14

"My mom and I go to the movies together and cry."

Kara, age 16

"I was shocked when I saw what Monica had drawn, because it was so violent and depressing. But I was glad she had taped it to the wall, because that meant she wasn't hiding her feelings."

mother of seventeen-year-old

"My painting is the way I express my real self."

Rebecca, age 18

"My creative writing is my way of telling others to accept me for who I am."

mother of five

"When I play the violin, I feel God singing inside me."

Mikatsu, age 13

"I draw a little angel and under it I write a short affirmation like, 'This angel brings you hope today,' and then I put it on her dresser. I don't do it every day, but I know she likes it because she's always asking me, 'Mom, where's my angel?' "

mother of thirteen-year-old

"Usually our first big snow occurs around the end of November, and I'm out there making a snowman.

My teenager thinks I'm crazy, but she always ends up helping me. She gets into it. It's our way of saying, 'Hello, winter.' "

mother of sixteen-year-old

"My mother taught me how to listen to music. Even though we like different kinds now, I still like listening with her."

Angela, age 10

"Ever since I was a little girl, my mom and I would make these wreaths to celebrate the seasons and other holidays. We use plants from nature and combine them with stuff around the house like ribbon and material, and then we hang them. Even though I live someplace else now, I still make them with her when I come home to visit."

Pam, age 19

"My middle daughter is a gardener like me. When we're creating our spring garden, I think we both feel a little closer to God even though we don't actually talk about it."

mother of three girls, ages 11, 13, and 18

How have you connected with your daughter through a shared creative activity?

REMEMBER THAT TIME WHEN WE BOTH . . .

When it comes to engaging in creativity with your daughter, it's often easier when she's a little girl than when she's a teenager. One reason is time. We *take* more time to be creative when our children are younger because, usually, they *have* more time. When our children are young, they're around us more, and since a young child's life is just naturally filled with magic and wonder, it's easier to connect through creativity with activities that capitalize on their imaginative powers. The connections came easier when we were little girls as well. I can remember, at age six, sitting with my mother on the front porch steps of my grandmother's house in Salt Lake City, Utah, making dye out of crushed pansy petals and then dyeing strips of cloth.

"My mother was a member of our church's altar guild. When I was in grade school I would go with her to decorate the altar with flowers for the Sunday service. If she let me arrange some flowers, I was in heaven. Especially when the pews would be full of people the next day all looking at my arrangement."

Deborah, age 48

"We used to make all sorts of pasta together. My mother was Italian, so for her, creativity started and ended in the kitchen. She was as religious about her cooking as she was about going to Mass."

Jennifer, age 52

"From the time I could walk, my mother would take me to her dance studio. If she wasn't giving classes, then I could put on the costumes and dance around."

Gloria, age 34

"When I was around four my mother would take me with her to her quilting circle. I would sit on the floor and make designs with the squares of material, and sometimes one of the women would sew some together for me for a doll blanket. I'm sure I get my love of weaving from that experience."

Doris, age 47

When you were a little girl, how did you and your mom or another person in your life do something creative together?

WHEN I WAS A LITTLE GIRL, MY _____ AND I CREATED . . .

My mother recalls how she created magic out of the commonplace when I was three years old:

We were stationed in Fayetteville, North Carolina, and you got very sick. The pediatrician said you had rheumatic fever, which at that time was dangerous because there were no antibiotics to fight it. You had to stay in bed, which was terribly hard for a three-year-old. So I got the idea of giving you a "mystery box." It was a shoe box filled with ordinary household items that changed every day. The game was that you had to make something out of the items. One day the box would hold corks, Popsicle sticks, some wooden spools, swatches of material, an empty toilet paper roll, a few crayons, and some Scotch tape. The next day there would be paper clips, string, a thimble, two chopsticks, an empty nose dropper, the cardboard from your father's laundered shirt, colored pencils, and some odd-shaped leaves. The "mystery box" was the best part of your day.

We should always be on the lookout for ways to create magical experiences out of the ordinary details of daily life. What creative activity did you do with your daughter when she was a little girl?

WHEN YOU WERE A LITTLE GIRL, WE USED TO . . .

If we make our everyday world more open to what is beautiful and imaginative, our relationships will open to the same.

When did *doing* something creative together make you feel closer to your daughter? It can be anything from cooking a special dish for dinner together, planning a garden, decorating for the holidays, painting a room in your house, or rearranging furniture.

WHEN WE DID

I FELT CLOSER TO YOU

However, most of us discover that when our daughters are older, opportunities to be creative together occur less often. In our family we met that challenge by establishing some traditions that fostered creativity when the girls were young. Then we were able to continue these traditions when they grew up.

For example, from preschool through high school, family gifts from both girls had to be handmade. It was perfectly fine if the gift was a little clunky because you had gravely overestimated your abilities in a certain medium such as origami, needlepoint, or woodworking. It was also okay to get help from family members other than the person who was receiving the gift. This collaboration was often the most connective part of the process since two (or, with particularly complicated gifts such as an illustrated book, three) people created together an expression of their love for the recipient.

The most meaningful creation is the annual wall calendar Julia and Emily make each year as a holiday gift for their father. The girls alternate drawing a picture for each month of the year celebrating some aspect of our family life. They use different mediums like paint, markers, pens, and pastels. It is their father's favorite gift of the season, and the collection of "calendars for Daddy" chronicles their perspective on life through the years.

Another way we are creative is when we arrange items on the top of a dresser, reconfigure a photograph display, or intentionally group objects on a bookshelf, entrance-hall table, kitchen windowsill, or desk.

What is on your dressing table or the top of your bureau?

I HAVE CHOSEN _____ TO PUT ON MY _____ . . .

WHAT IS CREATIVE ABOUT WHAT YOUR DAUGHTER
HAS CHOSEN TO PUT ON HER BUREAU OR BEDSIDE
TABLE?

Most of us associate spiritual creativity with faith traditions in which works of art or crafts are created for specific places of worship. We think of stained glass, religious

statuary, wall tapestries, altar cloths, an oratorio sung by a choir, chanting by Buddhist monks, or a Native American dance honoring Mother Earth.

We create altars through placement of special objects with the specific intention of connecting us with spirit and with one another. Peg Streep and Jean McMann, two authors who have written books about altars, say that the process of building an altar for ourselves makes us more aware of thoughts, emotions, and experiences from our past. As we search for those objects with special meaning, we make choices that are in themselves revealing about who we are.

Creating an altar for ourselves invites us to objectify what we hold sacred. We are asking ourselves to express our spirituality in physical form. The objects we choose are meaningful to us because they represent the spiritual in our lives.

"I would include a tuning fork that would represent my music, a quartz heart that represents God's love, my daughter's photo, a rose-scented candle, and two beautiful shells we found at the beach last summer because they remind me of nature and the ocean."

Ruth, age 49, mother of sixteen-year-old

"My altar would have the purple satin heart-shaped pillow with white lace that I got for Valentine's Day from my father when I was fifteen, lots of candles and lilacs, and a photograph of my baby."

Susan, age 26, mother of baby girl

"It would definitely be covered with red floral fabric, and it would have flowers on it and figurines of dogs and pictures of my daughters and me and of me growing up. An ornate cross would hang above."

Diane, age 52, mother of three girls

"My altar would have daffodils, crystal, candles, and water themes. And it would have one of my husband's flea-market finds like the little statue of Ganesh, the Hindu elephant god."

Carolyn, age 45, mother of fourteen-year-old

"I would hang a picture of the pietà, surround it with roses and candles, place a small crucifix in the center and, next to it, my rosary beads."

Anna, age 32, mother of two girls

"First and foremost it would be pink and green because those are my favorite colors, and it would have statues of angels. I would also have a vase of pink baby rosebuds on it, and lots of pictures of the people I love."

Amber, age 17

"My mom's picture, quotes I believe in, tiger's eye stones, lavender and rosemary growing in pots around it, rings with my birthstone, which is an opal, and my mother's birthstone, too, and my journal."

Linda, age 14

"I would have my pointe shoes on it, and pics of my pets, friends, family. I would decorate it with flowers and hang my favorite poster above it."

Cassie, age 12

"It would have a beautiful gold cross and some incense burning all the time. I would also put a candle on it and a polished stone I got last summer out West. There would be a special vase with fresh flowers that would change every day."

Angela, age 14

Where would your altar be, and what would you choose to put on it?

MY ALTAR WOULD BE . . .

What do you think your daughter might use to create her personal altar?

YOUR ALTAR WOULD INCLUDE . . .

Altars change with each discovery of new meaning in life or new glimpses of the sacred. They make us mindful of what is important to us spiritually. When we create them with our daughters, they connect us with each other. Whether we are acknowledging the personal resonance of an object from our past, the passage of an important event, the change of a season, or a beautiful memory, we are clarifying what brings us closer to each other.

What would you put on an altar you share with your daughter? What special objects do you both endow with sacred meaning? What events in both your lives might you want to celebrate and honor with symbols?

YOU AND I MIGHT CREATE AN ALTAR TOGETHER THAT WOULD INCLUDE . . .

If I Look as Closely as I Possibly Can

At a leaf or a petal or seed
If I stop what I'm doing to carefully observe
A grass blade, a clover, or reed
Then I see in the pattern, the color, the line
Of each stem or each root or each pod
How creation is part of my life here on earth
In each perfect fingerprint of God.

MORE PRAYERS ON MY PILLOW

May I awake with heartfelt joy, greeting th

Can you help me to be honest?

reality builds my strength in me

I'll reach out to heal with the truth

I'll reveal myself

I am I wish I could say what I go through I wish I could show my true soul I want to be real not perfect

Perfection takes too great a toll every lie

will make me strong I know what is right and wrong

will make me weaker every truth

Connecting with Truth

Can You Help Me to Be Truthful?

Reality builds strength in me.
I don't want to make up stories
Or wear a mask so you won't see.

Can you give me inner courage
To do what I know to be right?
With open heart I'll love you always
With honesty I'll win our fight.

MORE PRAYERS ON MY PILLOW

"I trust my mom because she'll always tell me the truth when I do something right and also when I do something stupid."

Tracy, age 14

"I tell them that as long as you tell me the truth, that's what counts, but if they tell me they have broken family rules, sometimes it's hard not to punish them."

Gretchen, age 44, mother of three teenage girls

"Sometimes it's really hard to tell the truth to your parents."

Laura, age 13

"I like it that my mom trusts me. She doesn't jump to conclusions about what I've been doing before I've told her like some of my friends' moms do.

Angie, age 16

"The truth is what I know to be right. That is a true fact that has helped me get through many difficult times in my life."

Janet, age 15

"I grew up on the saying that 'God only gives us what we can handle,' and that's what I believe to be the truth, so that's what I tell her when she gets upset about school."

Maureen, age 37, mother of fourteen-year-old

"In our house it's okay to have problems as long as you're honest about them."

Casey, age 10

"My inner truth is I've had a hard life and with God's help I still stand strong."

Rebecca, age 19

"My mother taught me to respect people who tell the truth."

Tawanna, age 15

"I want her to believe every day of her life that I will love her no matter what she does. That's the only truth that counts."

Helen, age 40, mother of sixteen-year-old

*W*hen Emily was in second grade and learning about King Arthur, she was asked to make a shield with her family crest and motto. Emily's motto was, "Sorry Don't Feed the Bulldog," a line from the television series *M*A*S*H*. My husband used the line when someone in our family crossed over another person's boundaries or did something selfish and then said, "I'm sorry." The assumption was that "I'm sorry" would get them off the hook although both parties knew it was not the truth. That was when the motto kicked in:

Emily:	"You wore my brown turtleneck again after I asked you not to, and now it's totally gross."
Julia:	"I'm sorry."
Emily:	"Sorry don't feed the bulldog."

Richard:	"You threw away my favorite T-shirt? You knew what that T-shirt meant to me. Even the *holes* had meaning."
Celia:	"I'm sorry."
Richard:	"Sorry don't feed the bulldog."

Celia:	"Why did you download all that music onto my laptop when the last time the computer crashed and I was an insane person for days?"
Emily:	"I'm sorry."
Celia:	"Sorry don't feed the bulldog."

Richard's goal was to encourage a more mindful response—one that took thought to culminate in an honest response. Like every family, our day-to-day lives include conflicts easily resolved with a truthful response, but often deflected with a lie. "I forgot." "I didn't mean to." "I didn't think you'd mind." "I got it confused."

Our motto is a gentle reminder of honesty without blowing the exchange out of proportion through accusation: "You're not sorry at all." "Are you calling me a liar?" "Yes." "Well, now you owe *me* an apology." And so on. When our girls are teens, it becomes even more important to strike a balance between parental control so rigid that any confrontation results in a self-defensive lie, and no accountability whatsoever. In other words, honesty with a light touch.

If you were going to make up a family motto that expressed an essential value for your family, what would it be?

OUR FAMILY MOTTO WOULD BE . . .

What would your family motto be if it addressed the value of truth?

OUR FAMILY MOTTO ABOUT TRUTH WOULD BE . . .

When we are controlling, we take so much personal responsibility for our daughter's life that we do not trust her to be responsible for it. In self-defense, she begins to distrust us and our connection with truth fragments. When a relationship built on trust transforms into one riddled with distrust, it becomes significantly weakened.

> "I wish I could tell my mother the truth about my eating disorder, but I don't trust her. She will take me to a doctor and I'll have to eat and not throw up."
>
> *Holly, age 17*

"My parents don't like my boyfriend so I don't tell them when I see him."

Sonya, age 14

"I cannot tell the truth to my mother about boys or sex. She would totally overreact."

Jillian, age 15

"I love her, but she doesn't give me my own space and she gets upset if I don't tell her every detail of what I do or I tell her she is prying too much."

Lydia, age 15

"I wish I could tell my mother that the truth is I am scared I'm going to die."

Kimberly, age 12

"I cannot talk to her about my true feelings because the people I would talk to I would not want to hurt, but sometimes it feels that no one can help me. And I get depressed."

Brittany, age 12

We can overcome our daughters' fears of telling us the truth by paying more attention to the truths we have in common. Being honest about the feelings and vulnerabilities that we share makes it easier to be honest about topics we don't agree on.

"My mom is opinionated about school things I tell her, but we pretty much agree on feelings."

Felicia, age 15

"I try to be honest with my kids, even if it makes me feel as though I look bad. I refuse to accept less than the truth from them, and if they are truthful, I don't betray their trust."

Joyce, age 42, mother of three girls ages 15, 17, and 20

"My mom and I can, like, go to a movie or watch a TV show and we are totally the same when it comes to what makes us laugh or cry. It's when we cry at the same time that really freaks me out, but in a good way."

Fiona, age 14

Every time we speak the truth—what we know in our hearts to be essentially right and good—we take one step closer to living truthfully.

How do you emphasize the importance of speaking the truth? For example, you might stress standing up for what you believe in as long as it does not infringe upon the rights of other people.

YOU AND I KNOW IT IS IMPORTANT TO SPEAK THE TRUTH BECAUSE . . .

Telling the truth is not always easy. However, lying is not so easy either, since it makes your life complicated, and you are always afraid you will be found out. Truth takes time, reflection, and often, tremendous courage, but it has distinct benefits: (1) Truth teaches you to pay attention. (2) Truth makes your life simpler. (3) Truth fosters trust and vice versa. (4) Truth feels good. (5) Truth pleases your soul.

"I think the best relationship is the one that you can be completely honest in and never regret telling the truth. You don't have to hold any feelings back."

Juliet, age 12

"Honesty and trust are the two more important ingredients when it comes to having a good relationship with your parents."

Chelsea, age 15

"I wish I had just one person I could trust enough to be completely truthful with. There is no one in my life who I can talk to and not be scared they'll think I'm stupid or something."

Alexandria, age 11

"Honesty. That's a hugely important character trait. Not being afraid of saying something important and that's meaningful to you for fear of being criticized."

Rhonda, age 16

If we are honest with each other, and if we keep integrity at the top of our values list, we trust each other. Truth and trust go hand in hand. When did you trust yourself and your daughter enough to speak the truth to her?

I TOLD YOU THE TRUTH WHEN I TOLD YOU ABOUT . . .

I CHOSE TO TELL YOU THAT BECAUSE . . .

Now think of a time when your daughter trusted you enough to tell you the truth.

REMEMBER WHEN YOU TOLD THE TRUTH ABOUT . . .

When we speak the truth we accept responsibility for being honest. As a result, we often avoid the truth in little ways. For years I was oblivious to the "little white lies" my daughters overheard me tell: To my mother: "I *love* the tropical bird placemats and napkins. I'm going to use them the next time I have people over for dinner." To Julia: "I swear to you, the only person who's going to notice your pimples is you." Or to Emily: "I'm not upset; I'm just tired."

Eventually I became aware of the impact these "little white lies" had on the girls. All lies weaken our connection with one another. If I could not tell Julia the truth about how she looked, why should she believe me when I told her she looked terrific and she really did? She began doubting me every time I gave her a compliment.

If I would not share my true feelings with Emily when she asked me if I was upset, why should she share her feelings with me? When was a time you told a "little white lie"?

ONE TIME I LIED WAS WHEN . . .

Our ability to use positive messages to strengthen and affirm our daughters' self-image is a precious gift. We want to respond positively, but at the same time we need to strike a balance so we're not "loose with the truth." If we are honest with our children, we will think twice about the words that come out of our mouths when we are talking to them.

Thinking twice about how I communicated with my daughters brought some changes to our relationship. Emily and I agreed that when something was wrong, we would share the truth about what we were feeling. Julia and I agreed that when either of us asked each other how we looked, we would get an honest answer. When did you tell the truth and receive a positive response from your daughter?

I TOLD YOU THE TRUTH ABOUT _____ , AND YOU _____ . . .

How has being truthful with each other strengthened your relationship?

BY BEING OPEN AND TRUTHFUL, WE HAVE . . .

Using truth to grow our daughters is one of the most powerful parenting tools we have. So we might be a little more mindful about *how* we communicate it. When we speak truthfully, our words are consistent with our tone, our facial expression, and our body language. When Julia and Emily were youngsters we would talk gibberish to each other, using only tone, facial expressions, and gestures to get our meaning across. It demonstrated how truth is often not in the words themselves, but in the way they are expressed.

We undercut ourselves by saying one thing with words and something totally different with our bodies. Which is the truth? Does our body language sometimes tell our daughters that we do not mean what we say?

WHEN DID YOU EXPRESS THE TRUTH TO YOUR
DAUGHTER WITH YOUR BODY IN A WAY THAT
CONTRADICTED YOUR WORDS?

In his book *Changes That Heal*, Dr. Henry Cloud points out that, "Truth is what is real; it describes how things really are. God's truth leads us to what is real, to what is accurate." We need to discover what is true and use it to "shape" real and authentic relationships with our daughters. We can live our own lives truthfully and teach by example. The more we honor the truth, the more our daughters will.

How has living your own life truthfully brought you closer to your daughter?

YOU HAVE SEEN ME BE TRUTHFUL ABOUT . . .

Often we discover the most profound truths about ourselves through our children. These truths may not be what we anticipated, are prepared for, or even want to know, but they are always connecting and healing if we are open to hearing them.

One truth about myself that I learned from my daughters is that I am impatient. They pointed my impatience out to me with so many stark examples that I finally accepted their teaching. Now I realize how much I missed of their childhood because I was so impatient to move on to the next activity.

What truth have you learned about yourself your daughter?

YOU TAUGHT ME THAT I AM . . .

Write three phrases that are true about yourself. These truths may or may not be news to your daughter. It does not matter, because what is important is that now she will know you consider them important because you wrote them down.

HERE ARE THREE TRUTHS ABOUT ME:

1.

2.

3.

What three truths could you list about your daughter?

THREE TRUTHS ABOUT YOU ARE:

1.

2.

3.

To Everyone Else I'm Creative and Bold

To everyone else I'm quite fine
To the outside world success is my game
To the outside world luck is mine.

But they don't understand what is happening inside
They don't detect the confusion.
They don't know what I go through alone
The struggle I have with illusion.

I wish I could say what I feel
I wish I could show my true soul
I want to be real, not pretending
Pretending takes too great a toll.

MORE PRAYERS ON MY PILLOW

EIGHT

Connecting with Laughter

My Self Does Not Recognize Boundaries

My self will not stay in the box.
My self is not fond of orderly lines
Restrictions, prescriptions, constrictions, or fines.
My self cannot stand chains or locks.

My self is a child and a prankster.
My self likes unconventional means.
My self enjoys work when it feels like play
Joking, provoking, invoking all day
My self loves to laugh in my dreams.

MORE PRAYERS ON MY PILLOW

*L*aughing together:

"My mother and I used to laugh when we watched cartoons. Now we laugh when we watch *Friends* or *The Simpsons*."

Jeanine, age 15

"My mom and I laugh about how clueless boys are. Like how they have no idea how girls are, like, two steps ahead of them. We come up with some pretty funny examples, because of my two older brothers."

Nancy, age 14

"My mom always sees the humorous side of things, even when I am seriously stressed. Once when someone stole my backpack, she described how disappointed the person would be when they found all the rotten sandwiches and gum wrappers and broken pens and other junky stuff I carry around. It was pretty funny except I never got my backpack back."

Kelly, age 13

"Mostly it's when we go clothes shopping that my mother and I laugh. She holds up something outrageous like a pink thong as if she thinks it's perfect for her, and I crack up."

Vanessa, age 16

"When I was a little girl my mother and I used to tell knock-knock jokes to each other. We still do sometimes even if they are stupid."

Leah, age 11

"It's a family joke that I'm so forgetful. So sometimes I jot down funny 'Mom's Lists' and post them on the refrigerator, like: Remember you have four children. Or: Take shoes off before going to bed. Or: Don't forget where you live. We all need to be able to keep perspective on life."

Catherine, age 45, mother of two girls, ages 8 and 10

Laughing apart:

> "My sense of humor is the same, but my daughters' humor has changed. They used to think it was funny when I cracked a joke, but now they just roll their eyes. I wish we could laugh together again."
>
> *Martha, age 50, mother of two girls, ages 13 and 17*

> "I can't think of a time me and my mom laugh. She doesn't think anything I do is funny."
>
> *Gillie, age 12*

> "I only laugh with my friends."
>
> *Susanne, age 11*

> "My parents are too serious to laugh much. When I'm around them, I'm serious, too."
>
> *Sheila Ann, age 12*

When Julia was three, I made up a silly song to sing each day when I drove her the mile or so to a nursery school summer camp. She was always tearful, certain she was going to have a miserable time, which she seldom did; certain she would hate whatever I had packed in her brown bag lunch, which she never did; and certain I would not come to fetch her home, which I always did. The song, which was essentially tuneless, had to do with bunnies and went something like, "Julia loves baby bunnies. They play play play all day. They dance and sing and poop on the ground and then they run away." The verses were endless and got progressively more ridiculous as we closed in on the camp, so that by the time we pulled into the parking lot, Julia and the bunnies had done everything a three-year-old could possibly consider funny, and Julia was beside herself with laughter. This inane song was even more useful when, ten years later, she came home in tears because all the "popular" girls cold-shouldered her at lunch. After holding her tight, I then suddenly burst forth with the bunny song and we both began to giggle.

What silly ritual or funny phrase did you do with your daughter when she was little?

WHEN YOU WERE LITTLE, WE USED TO LAUGH TOGETHER WHEN I . . .

How might you use the same humor to connect with your daughter today?

THESE DAYS WE STILL LAUGH WHEN . . .

Most of us take life too seriously. We have forgotten how to relax and look for the humor in our circumstances. When we laugh together, our inner selves are released from the confines of our public persona and, in that moment of laughter, we connect.

No matter how we try to control it, life is going to surprise us, often in absurd ways. Acceptance of our human condition does not have to make us hopeless, bitter, or cynical. Seeing the humor in our daily lives can strengthen and sustain us with new perspective and balance.

Instead of working so hard to get life right, laughter makes me see that life is already right, and I just have to trust its rightness. Giving up control over life is not easy for most of us, yet when we do, we become a little less self-absorbed. When we are able to share our humorous perspective on life with our daughters, we give them a little perspective and balance as well.

When did you help your daughter gain a little perspective about life by pointing out the humor of her situation?

REMEMBER WHEN I GOT YOU TO LAUGH ABOUT . . .

When did *both* of you laugh because the same thing struck you as funny?

REMEMBER WHEN WE BOTH STARTED LAUGHING
AT . . .

Laughing at ourselves with an understanding of how silly we can sometimes be is a deeply spiritual response to life that we all might practice more often. Being ourselves is often silly or outrageous, but it is also infinitely more appealing to others than the guarded self who is usually predictable, defensive, and serious. If we cannot be ourselves we end up fearful. We worry that other people might laugh judgmentally, with derision or scorn, if we drop our guard.

Nourishing our childlike sense of humor and fostering it in our daughters enables us both to better cope with the process of living. When our girls are younger, laughter is a natural occurrence, woven into their lives. Our task is to retrieve these humorous moments from childhood and use them as connections when times get tough later on.

"My mom lost her job one time and I was afraid she would be angry and sad. But instead, she asked each of us to tell her something we *didn't* like about her working. It was pretty much fun because we got to tell her stuff like we didn't like it that she was so crabby every morning. My brother told her he hated it that whenever he called her she was in a meeting and talked in a whisper. Then she made us tell her what we would like about her being fired. I said that I thought she would look better because she wouldn't be so tired all the time and it's better when she doesn't wear lots of makeup like my history teacher, Mrs. Wilson, who has to hide her age under foundation."

Becky, age 10

"I must admit I don't do many childish things anymore. I'm extremely busy with my law practice, and my kids are all teenagers. But I do remember a time this winter when my two oldest talked me into going sledding with them. They had me sit in this saucer thing and then they pushed me down the hill. I laughed all the way down. We must have been there for a couple hours."

Victoria, age 50

"Well, the person I laugh with the most is my mother, who is eighty. She can still make me laugh about myself whenever I'm blue. She just reminds me of something I did or she did a long time ago that was funny, and we both start laughing."

Diana, age 45

My husband and I treasure the times when we laugh with our daughters now that they are teenagers. I try to commit them to memory, these sudden outbursts, when we all, at the same instant, recognize the humor of the moment. Our family acted silly a lot when the girls were younger, so we have a rich repertoire of silliness to draw on:

- *Making "bunny ears" above a person's head when he or she is acting pretentious, overly serious or, best of all, on camera.*
- *Walking into a wall, pretending to hit your forehead while kicking the wall with your foot to make a hitting noise, and then staggering backward as if dizzy.*
- *Suddenly breaking into a goofy walk, face, song, or excerpt from memorized dialogues of silly Monty Python routines, such as "The Spanish Inquisition."*

"The best times I have with my mom are when we're watching television together and there's something funny on and we're both laughing."

Allison, age 13

"I have reservations about some of the programs my daughters watch on television, but I try to relate to a couple of their favorites, like *Friends*, because it's an opportunity to relax with them instead of us always fighting."

Helen, age 50, mother of two girls, ages 13 and 16

"I am appalled at what is made available for children to watch on television these days. We have fairly strict rules about what they can and cannot watch. On the other hand, one night my thirteen-year-old daughter's friend brought over a video of the movie *Clueless*, and the three of us laughed the entire time."

Rose Marie, age 42

"My mom likes *Sleepless in Seattle*. She makes me watch it with her, like, all the time. At first I was like, why? But now I have to admit it's pretty funny."

Tammy, age 11

Can you name two favorite television programs, videos, or movies that you and your daughter still watch and laugh at together?

YOU AND I LAUGH WHEN WE WATCH . . .

We can also teach our daughters how to put setbacks into perspective, and how to laugh at the fact that life is what it is. Most of us have become masters at laughing at life's little ironies, and irony often works well with teenagers who like to think of themselves as even more jaded ("been there, done that") than we are.

A little more world-weary than when our daughters were toddlers, we shake our heads in mock despair over junk e-mail; endless "to do" lists; ever again purchasing a bathing suit; the boss's irrational need to micromanage; the amount of money we spend on our daughters' makeup, clothes, summer camps, extracurricular sports, and CDs;

our own outdated wardrobe consisting primarily of different shades and lengths of monochromatic jackets and skirts; the last time we had a romantic weekend with the man in our life, the last time we had a man in our life.

We joke to our teenage daughters, saying, "It figures I would have a fender bender one week before the lease is up. How else would I be able to pay the extra one thousand dollars to give my car back to the dealer?" "Of course the basement flooded while we were away on vacation. If it had flooded when we were home, then we'd have had to stress over trying to save all the carpeting and books that we can now simply throw away." "Now that you've lost your favorite fleece, I guess you'll finally be able to wear the jacket we bought you last month."

Pick a time you laughed ironically.

REMEMBER WHEN I LAUGHED IRONICALLY AT . . .

Episcopal priest Tilden Edwards says in *Sabbath Time*, "Laughter is a special kind of play. Laughter can be escapist, contrived, or cynical, but not when it is God laughing through us. Then it is a simply restful celebration of the life that is. Such laughter is schoolmaster, too. It teaches us humility and deflates pretension." Since life is what it is, we will always have opportunities to make "light of things" with our daughters. Even in the most profound circumstances we can look for the humor in order to find our balance.

"Me and my mother started laughing in synagogue one time because it was so amazing that, just at the point when the rabbi said, '. . . and God said, let there be light,' light came in through the window and lit up the podium like God was a lighting director or something."

Rebecca, age 14

"When my older sister got married in our backyard, my mom was crying, like, before the music started. Halfway through the ceremony my sister took the handkerchief out of her boyfriend's (he wasn't her husband yet) pocket and walked over and gave it to my mom. It cracked both of them up."

Trish, age 19

"When my grandfather died, they had this memorial service where everyone who wanted to could get up and tell stories about him and them. Some of them were so funny, it made my heart feel good again."

Tiffany, age 12

"At my daughter's graduation from high school last year, she was wearing a long white dress, and when she went up to the stage to receive her diploma from the principal, I began to cry. Then my youngest son, who is four, asked, 'Mommy, are you crying because Whitney is going to marry that strange man?' Suddenly my tears became tears of laughter."

Nancy, age 45

When did you laugh with your daughter during a significant life event?

REMEMBER WHEN WE WERE BOTH AT _____ AND WE LAUGHED BECAUSE _____ . . .

My former yoga teacher, Alexandra, an ageless, beautiful woman who lights up any room she enters, invited us to laugh for five minutes early on in our sessions. We are an assorted bunch: women of varying ages, body types, and stages of expertise in our practice (from beginners like myself who still have trouble with sitting cross-legged, to advanced students who could sit for an hour in "spinal twist" without whimpering). But every one of us is an expert at laughing. We start out sounding rather forced, because there's nothing to laugh about. Soon, however, contagious laughter takes over, and we are giggling, guffawing, snorting, and finally, roaring with huge belly laughs that roll us around on our mats until we are exhausted and pause for breath, which is always the moment when someone starts laughing again and the whole process repeats itself. At the

instant Alexandra tells us to stop, there is a moment of connectedness between us all.

"I have a group of 'sisters,' and every time we get together all we do is laugh. I don't know what about exactly. Everything, I guess. Men, kids, sex, our weight,
our work, whatever."

Arlethia, age 51

"When we have sleepovers, me and my three best
friends stay up all night watching television and telling jokes and stuff. One night we laughed so hard, I
threw up."

Olivia, age 11

"When I'm baby-sitting my little brother, sometimes
he does these things that are totally gross but just
crack me up, like when he follows right behind me
and burps."

Vickie, age 13

"I laugh with my best friend from high school the
same way we did way back then."

Sonya, age 43

"When I'm with my friends, all we do is sit around and laugh."

Katie, age 16

Who is someone in your life who you laughed with or laugh with now?

I LAUGH WITH . . .

My daughter and I had an opportunity to see the humor in a situation and, from that experience, shared, for a moment, a sense of the spiritual in our lives. We were jogging around the local high school track one Saturday morning after a rainstorm. The track borders a grassy playing field. We saw three burly ground maintenance men sitting motionless on their oversized mowing vehicles, all staring at the same spot in the field. They had cut the grass to form a perfect circle around a pool of rainwater and were now waiting patiently. Leisurely enjoying all that the pool had to offer on a warm spring morning were a pair of mallard ducks and their four ducklings. Judging by the family's watery enthusiasm, it was going to be a long wait, yet there was an element of mutual respect between the men and these wild creatures that filled the heart. Every time we ran close to the man-versus-duck standoff at the pool of water, we laughed.

"One time when my mom picked me up from school, I was, like, so stressed out, and she was stressed out, and we started yelling at each other, and then we both noticed this amazing perfect sunset that looked like a cartoon. We saw it at the same time and we just started laughing because it was so beautiful."

Shawna, age 15

"I can't talk to my mother about my problems with sex and boys, but sometimes when we're joking around she'll tell me something she did when she was my age that was totally outrageous, and I'll go, 'Mom, shut up. I don't want to hear about it.' So even though I can't really talk to her, at that moment I feel like I have talked to her because of what she said."

Kelly, age 14

"We laugh all the time about the most ordinary things, like the dog being scared of waves at the beach because he thinks they're alive."

Megan, mother of three girls, ages 11, 14, and 15

"After my mom and I joke around, I feel so much better, but it's hard to explain why."

Britanee, age 13

Let Me Take from This Moment

Just one memory I can treasure
When everything came together
In the brilliance of the day.

Let me capture joyous laughter
How I felt and how I acted
So when all else is subtracted
I'll recall I felt this way.

Let me throw off all my burdens
Inhale deeply all the magic
Use it when there's something tragic
When I'm lost or gone astray.

MORE PRAYERS ON MY PILLOW

May I have the courage to start over again; May I reach deep down to my core

what I'm aiming for. May I have the strength

May I have the courage to play for high stakes because that's what I'm aiming for. May I have the strength

to face down loss; May I push past all of my fears to aim for the heart

NINE

Connecting with Courage

I Am Not Helpless

I am not weak
I will not shatter
I will not weep
I stand alone
And I stand strong
I can be me
Without being wrong.

PRAYERS ON MY PILLOW

At first the Self speaks in an almost inaudible whisper. It may feel like a soft, gentle nudge, or it can be seen in the mind's eye as a fleeting image. . . . You get it, then lose it, then you reclaim it again, until you finally lock on. . . . As you begin to trust the wisdom of the Self, you will have the compass you need to sail north on stormy seas.

ROMANCING THE SHADOW: A GUIDE TO
SOUL WORK FOR A VITAL, AUTHENTIC LIFE,
BY CONNIE ZWEIG AND STEVE WOLF

"If I tell my mom that there is something I really want to do, she encourages me to go for it. Like when I tried out for this play, I was stressed because I never acted before, but my mom kept telling me to audition even if I didn't get a part. Guess what? I got a part, and now I have a part in another play."

Brenda, age 13

"I try to show her how to make responsible decisions. I know that means that sometimes she'll fail, and that is hard. But if she can't learn to trust herself to make the right choices, how is she going to do when she goes out on her own?"

Ruth, mother of seventeen-year-old

"My mom lets me pick the activities I want to do instead of forcing me to do ones I don't want to, except she still makes me follow the rules, like you have to do your homework first."

Jennie, age 11

"I am willing to back her in all her endeavors. No matter how she does, I concentrate on her strengths, not her weaknesses, but in return, I expect her to live by the values she has learned at home and at church."

Ivory, mother of sixteen-year-old

"My mother is always telling people that she learns more from me than anyone else in her life. That makes me feel soooooo good."

Sue Ann, age 10

"I want her to believe in herself. She is so intelligent and has so many talents, and she is always putting herself down. I try to talk to her, but she doesn't want to listen."

Paula, mother of fourteen-year-old

"I am from the Cheyenne River Sioux tribe in South Dakota. I am so proud of being born on an Indian reservation. I wouldn't change it for anything."

Marie, age 12

"My mother makes me get up to go to open gyms in the morning for basketball. These are pretty early, and most times I'd rather be sleeping, but she knows how much I want to get good at basketball. By the time we get there, I'm glad she woke me up."

Shonnita, age 15

*A*fter watching a *Sesame Street* segment featuring Itzhak Perlman, Julia, who was then three, decided she wanted to play the violin. I was skeptical until two years later, when I found a drawing in her backpack entitled "My Dream." It was a Magic Marker self-portrait of herself playing the violin. I started researching music teachers the next day.

Her father and I listened to the ten variations on "Twinkle Twinkle Little Star" from *Suzuki Book One*, scratched out on a quarter-size fiddle until I found myself climbing every flight of stairs to the exact pacing of the "Twinkles" on her metronome. For ten years she practiced, performed alone and in orchestras, played for sheer pleasure, created original compositions, and entertained us by taking requests. Her father's favorite was the theme from the Ken Burns *Civil War* television series; mine was the movie theme from *The Last of the Mohicans*. Then, at fifteen, she stopped playing.

Ultimately the violin could not compete with academics, year-round athletics, and a social life. We never said a word about her decision or the fact that, for the next three years, the violin did not come out of its case. Was the time and energy she had invested in weekly lessons (she had made it through *Suzuki Book Seven*), practice sessions, recitals, orchestral concerts, and string ensembles, not to mention the money we had spent on increasingly expensive instruments and increasingly longer lessons, wasted?

Let us see: She developed a love of music that she will forever treasure as a way to express herself. She learned what it takes in terms of hard work and pure fortitude to stand alone in front of a hundred people, overcome stage fright, and focus on playing a complicated and long violin composition with enough passion that no one looked at their watches. She realized, in middle school, that some of those girls she wanted to impress the most didn't consider playing the violin a particularly cool thing to do. She would have to choose between playing furtively or playing defiantly. She chose the latter. She found out that there were an incredible number of young violinists far better than she was, and if competition was her only game, she would and did lose. Most of all, she discovered the courage to be herself.

There may be no lesson in life more important than learning to be ourselves. Armed with self-knowledge and self-worth, we can act fearlessly, with confidence and power. We connect with courage whether it is through work, creative endeavors, sports, romance, parenting, or reaching out to help others in our community.

How does your daughter express her courage to be herself? Is it through her choice of music, room décor, athletics, academic subjects, appearance, relationships, practice of her faith, creative endeavors, or something else entirely?

YOU DEMONSTRATE COURAGE TO BE YOURSELF
WHEN . . .

Over the years, in what ways have you supported your
daughter's determination to be herself? Validating her hopes,
dreams, strengths, unique talents, and ability to act respon-
sibly is what gives her courage.

I SUPPORT YOUR DESIRE TO . . .

When we have the courage to be ourselves, we are more able to make responsible decisions until choosing wisely and well becomes second nature. We take risks, are open to new ideas, and maintain our independence from the crowd if joining it will jeopardize what we know to be right.

As adults, most of us find that we still avoid taking responsibility for some parts of our lives, through avoidance, lethargy, habit, or fear. For instance, do we, as adults, have the courage to be ourselves when it comes to money? Managing our money wisely and well may not be a life lesson we learn in childhood, but unless we learn it sometime, there is a good chance we're going to be distracted from our spiritual parenting by issues of survival. No matter how much money we have, we can be certain that our daughters will watch us make personal choices about money that reveal how much courage we have to be who we are.

> "After my dad left us, my mom had to go to work to support me and my sister. It seems like all she worries about is money and how we have to be careful. I never thought about money being so important and all until now. Could you write a prayer for her so she won't be so scared?"
>
> *Katherine, age 11*

"My mom taught our family about tithing in church and how important it is to remember those people in the world who have a lot less money than you do."

Hannah, age 19

"I know my parents cheat on their taxes, because they always boast about it."

Lucinda, age 11

"My mother and I fight over money. All she does is tell me I spend too much or I spend it on the wrong stuff, but I watch her spend money on the same things she criticizes me for, like getting her nails done or new clothes."

Tammie, age 14

"I don't think it's fair that my stepdad gives my younger brother a bigger allowance than me and my mother never says a word. It's like he controls the money in our family."

Megan, age 12

"I wish my mother would be honest with me about our money troubles. She tells me everything is fine, but I know it isn't. I don't mind that we have to cut back on a lot of things. What makes me angry is that she is treating me like a child."

Celeste, age 16

Whether we are deciding how to make money, budget it, spend it, save it, invest it, or donate a portion of it to those who have less, we have opportunities to communicate long-lasting messages about materialism, independence, common sense, responsibility, generosity, balance, and courage. Can we use the topic of money to reinforce courage? Of course. We all know that if we want to get our teenage daughters to talk to us, we can always bring up the subject of money. Suddenly you have her full attention. We can use this attention-getter to generate a greater self-confidence in her own abilities. For instance, we could say, "What if you had an increase in your allowance along with an increase in being responsible for what you spend on yourself . . . ?" Or, "I'd like your advice on what we should do with our United Way contribution this year. . . ." Or, "Here's an offer: Grandma gave you twenty-five dollars, which you can spend any way you like. However, I'll add five dollars to that amount for more beads to make your jewelry."

How does your daughter spend money in a way that strengthens her sense of self-worth?

YOU SPEND YOUR MONEY ON . . .

My husband and I decided that once they became teenagers, our girls would get summer jobs. Instead of simply observing the working world, they entered it. Julia worked in a clothing store during the day and then, once she was older, added a second part-time job working for a catering company at night. Emily worked at the local recreational club, first running the concession stand, which required her to have home-made baked goods behind the counter by 8 A.M., and then later as a desk clerk.

Through interaction with supervisors, fellow workers,

and customers, they learned the values of empathy, honesty, responsible behavior, grace, discretion, and the importance of keeping your word. The three of us found new ways to connect with spirit each time we reflected on work-related questions such as:

- *How do you keep your integrity but, at the same time, honor the rule that "the customer is always right"?*
- *How much can you learn about people's spiritual side by observing their spending behavior?*
- *Why does it take so much courage to ask your boss for a raise when you honestly believe you are worth more than he is paying you?*
- *If "it's all about money," how much room can there be for happiness?*
- *If you just work for money but not for love of the work itself, why do you so quickly lose your enthusiasm? What has to happen for you to dread work?*
- *And finally, is there a way to work and not have it resemble school? Didn't the person who invented "nine to five" or "seven to three-thirty" know that spiritual time has nothing to do with schedules?*

How do you and your daughter deal with issues of self-worth, integrity, and courage within the context of working?

WE TALK ABOUT HOW WHEN YOU WORK . . .

Parenting experts advocate acting with courage and conviction in front of your children so they will literally see how the most important person in their lives values self-worth.

> "Once I went to my mom's company on 'Take Your Daughter to Work Day' and it was, like, pretty cool the way she did this PowerPoint presentation and everyone listened."
>
> *Samantha, age 10*

"I'll never forget the time Jennifer and I were at a gas station, and one of the mechanics was giving this elderly woman a hard time about her car, confusing her, and talking to her as if she were a child. Finally I couldn't stand it any longer, and I went over and said, 'I couldn't help overhearing what you just said to this woman. I may know very little about cars, but I do know about customer service, and you were just unbelievably rude to this customer. I think you owe her an apology.' After we drove away, Jenny said, 'Mom, that was awesome how you stuck up for that lady.' And I said, 'You would have done the same thing, honey.' "

Eve, age 46, mother of Jennifer, age 10

"My mother is an artist. She paints the most amazing pictures, and people all want to buy them. But sometimes, if she really likes the picture, she won't sell it to them even if we need the money. I admire her for that."

Nina, age 15

"I would say my mom has the most self-confidence of anyone I know. She is a policewoman. She risks her life to help people. Once, when she was off duty, we rode around in a patrol car together, and I couldn't believe how all the people on the street knew her and said hi with big smiles and all. I know she loves her job."

Rolita, age 13

Describe a time when you've role-modeled assertiveness to your daughter.

I WAS ASSERTIVE AND COURAGEOUS WHEN I . . .

We can role-model courage to be ourselves by simply supporting what our daughters want to be. What we have in common with our girls need not be the specific activity, hope, or dream, but the yearning for self-expression combined with the courage to fulfill it.

"I am athletic, friendly, and helpful. My dream is to become a trapeze artist in a circus. My mom found me a gymnastics teacher who teaches trapeze. I am the only kid in my school who is learning trapeze, which makes me feel proud."

Frannie, age 13

"I hope that someday I can become a musical-comedy actress. I know everyone, including my parents, says it's very competitive and hard to make a living on the stage, but I want to try. I've been taking dance and singing lessons. This year I was the lead in *Guys and Dolls* at our high school, and I'm going to apply to colleges that have good theater departments."

Abby, age 18

"Someday I am going to own a stable and give horse-back lessons to disabled kids just like the teachers do who work at the place where I ride."

Denise, age 11

"My mom supported me throughout my entire basketball career, no matter how much driving she had to do to get me to the games on time. She would even take off from work. I am now in ninth grade and just made the varsity team. I am the only ninth grader on the team. Now I have a chance to show my mom how good I can be."

Jackie, age 15

"When I told my mom I wanted to be a photographer, she said that as long as I took photos, she would find some way to buy me the film and get them developed."

Bernice, age 16

"My dream is to be the best woman soccer player in the world."

Vickie, age 10

What hopes and dreams of your daughter's do you support and nourish?

I SUPPORT YOUR DREAM OF . . .

When I was growing up, I wanted to be a ballet dancer. My mother provided lessons for me from the time I was five until I was sixteen. She took me to lessons two or three times a week, made costumes, and sat through rehearsals, but kept her own concerns about ballet as my chosen career to herself: "Ballet was very important to you. You even rather seriously considered going off to study dance when you got a chance your junior year in high school. I wanted you to stay in high school and go to college, but I didn't say no. Instead, I helped you look at all sides of the decision and left it pretty much up to you to make up your own mind. It was a tempting choice to you, and we realized this. I was relieved when you decided not to go."

When you were your daughter's age, what were your hopes and dreams?

MY HOPES AND DREAMS WERE TO . . .

When I was young, I avoided every athletic activity I could because I was afraid that if I risked trying it, I would fail. In retrospect this was sad, because, for example, I never learned to swim. When walking along the beach, if ocean waves occasionally come up to my ankles, I skip up the beach a foot or two, irrationally worried that I will be swept away. If the waves hit my knees, I panic.

However, when Julia and Emily came along, I was

determined they would have the opportunity to make athletics a part of their lives if they chose to do so. I made sure they had swimming lessons and, thanks to Richard, learned to "throw like a boy." As a result, because my husband took a keen interest in developing his daughters' athletic abilities, and our schools now offer girls such a variety of individual and team sports to choose from, both Julia and Emily developed into fine athletes. They take great pleasure in playing year-round sports, including volleyball, basketball, lacrosse, tennis, and swimming. They took *such* great pleasure that I found myself on the sidelines while the rest of the family went diving for rings in the deep end of the community swimming pool or played tennis at the local park.

I went to my daughters' volleyball, basketball, and lacrosse games, and tried to relate to the experience of being an athlete by being a sympathetic listener when they lost, or a credible champion when they won. I always cheered loudly even though it was usually at the wrong moment for the wrong reason.

In my early forties I decided that, together with my daughters, we would all give skiing a try. I am originally from Salt Lake City, Utah, and my parents live near Alta, a ski resort, so it seemed logical to travel to ski country one spring vacation with Julia and Emily. Each morning we went to ski school and each afternoon we skied.

The girls took to skiing like ducks to water, progressing rapidly from beginners to intermediates in two days. They progressed so quickly that my vision of us all skiing together or grouped fetchingly for a photo op at the top of the mountain with our goggles on our heads, wearing brightly colored parkas never materialized. I did not see them until it was time to go home. I started at stage two of five different beginners' levels and never got beyond it. I could not relax my body enough to get into the rhythm of skiing, and I was not coordinated enough to use the skis and poles properly. Getting on and off the lifts was terrifying. Plus, it was cold.

However, I kept at it, meeting friendly beginners who would, the next day, be on intermediate trails while I retraced my route down the same stage-two trail. I had written off the entire experience as a disaster when, on the last afternoon of the last day, Emily asked me to ski with her. She convinced me to take the easiest of the intermediate trails, and so I did, trusting in her ability to get me down in one piece. My life was in her hands.

We started down what seemed to be the longest and most harrowing trail on the mountain, and I immediately fell down. Emily patiently skied back and helped me up. We started off a second time. Slowly we made our way down the mountain, Emily talking me through each turn, gradation, and rough spot and yelling encouragement like, "Yo, Mom, you're doin' great," or, "You can make it, just go slow." When we had completed the run, we were both beaming. "Mommy, that was the bravest thing you've ever done," Emily said. "I know how scared you were, 'cause I've felt the same way."

"I've tried to be a role model for my daughter by showing her I have the courage to take risks. For example, last year I left my full-time job to start my own bakery business. My daughter was very proud of me. I think it has made us much closer when she sees what I'm going through to get it off the ground, and yet I never give up."

Carol Ann, age 50

"Setting high standards for myself has made a difference in how my girls approach what they do. They want to achieve at what they do as I have. I think, for women, it's important to demonstrate how important it is to have self-confidence that you can be the best."

Yvonne, age 45

"I try to show my daughter that the way to live life is to the best of your ability. Even if it means you fail sometimes, always have faith that God wants you to be who you are. I am a single mom of three children, and I had to learn this lesson late in life. I want her to learn it early."

Ann, age 40

In what ways do you role-model courage to your daughter?

I HAVE SHOWN MY COURAGE TO YOU BY . . .

Helping our daughters have the courage to be themselves empowers us both. However, we need to be mindful that we're helping them to be themselves and not to be what they *think* we want them to be, which is often "perfect." We need to remind them that no one is perfect. The very nature of being ourselves makes everyone a misfit in one way or another. Perfection is not possible. However, with all the contradictory messages our society sends adolescent girls, it takes courage *not* to strive to be perfect.

For example, girls are *told* "looks don't matter," but then *see* girls who are thin and beautiful featured in the media with all the trappings of success, from the cute boyfriend to the ideal car. Girls are *told* "grades aren't the only thing in life," but then *learn* that if they don't have a high grade point average and lots of extracurricular activities, they may not get into the "right" college. Girls are *told* "you should be assertive," but then *discover* if "assertive" means being crabby, argumentative, or standing up for what they believe in, they must pipe down and not make waves.

I remember speaking at length to a friend of my daughter's, a beautiful, talented, and intelligent girl filled with spirit in the best sense of the word, who sobbed in anguish because she was not accepted to the college of her dreams. She felt that she had failed her family, her school, and most of all, herself. The fact that she had been accepted to three excellent colleges, any one of which would give her a wonderful life experience, entirely escaped her. The process had had a negative impact on her soul and the soul of her family. And the pressure this young girl experienced can start as early as preschool.

> "No matter what I do, it seems like I can't please my mother. She's always saying I can do better. If I get a B, she asks why didn't I make an A."
>
> *Kimberly, age 12*

"I'm under a lot of pressure right now because I have to make good grades on my finals, and also our soccer team is in the championships. I am the goalie. That means I cannot make any mistakes."

Polly, age 11

"Please write me a prayer, because I am so depressed. I did real bad on my grades this semester and now I am grounded. Plus, I gained a lot of weight and hate the way I look now. I just want to die."

Crystal, age 14

"My parents act like they wanted a perfect child but they got me instead."

Gretchen, age 13

"I am friendly, helpful, energetic, and loving, but I have some problems. First of all, I am big for my age and don't look so good. Second, I have what they call attention disorder. I wish more people would appreciate me for my good qualities instead of my bad ones."

Hillary, age 11

What do you love about your daughter's courage to be herself?

I LOVE YOU FOR YOUR COURAGE TO BE . . .

Our daughters willingly, happily, and spiritually try to please us, whether it is applying to kindergarten, auditioning for the school play, attempting a goal for their junior soccer team, getting an A on a book report, or seeking admission to college. We are grateful for their trust in our demands that they take risks; dare to dream; try just a little bit harder; shake off defeat; give it their all.

Yet it is difficult to walk that tightrope between wanting the very best for our children—basically setting the bar higher for them than our parents did for us—and foisting on them hopes and goals that cause them needless anxiety and fear that they will disappoint us. We need to connect with courage in ways that help them be themselves.

So let us think clearly, carefully, and most of all spiritually about the messages we send our daughters regarding the courage to be themselves. When our daughters are often their own severest critics, when society urges them to compete and excel across the board, when their time is organized into schedules that no adult could sustain, courage is exactly what is needed. We both need courage to be who we are and then to take pride in that person in all her glory.

I Define Myself with Words

Of strength and beauty.
I show myself with acts
Of grace and loving.
I humor myself with smiles
Of laughter and pleasure.
I guide myself with dreams
Of greatness and giving.
I soothe myself with whispers
Of caring and healing.
I treat myself with hopes
Of happiness and winning.
I grow myself with courage
Of feeling and knowing.

PRAYERS ON MY PILLOW

May every day I live be graced with love

I hold a secret in my heart and the secret is love

The gift life

I see a dream inside my mind and the dream is love

I feel the warmth around

the warmth is

and the gift is love

I feel the warmth around

Connecting with Love

I Hold a Secret in My Heart

And the secret is love.
I hear a whisper in my ear
And the whisper is love.
I see a dream inside my mind
And the dream is love.
I take the gift life offers
And the gift is love.
I feel God's warmth around me
And the warmth is love.

MORE PRAYERS ON MY PILLOW

"My parents, God, my grandfather, and my best friend, Ryan, love me."

Stacie, age 11

"My most treasured belief is that my family loves me for myself."

Rachel, age 10

"My mother tells me to look at other people with love because that may be the only love that others see each day."

Hannah, age 15

"Love bubbles up inside me when I am singing a song that I really like, or sometimes when I pray."

Lisa, age 13

"I don't look at it as making it through her teen years. That means I'm loving her in spite of the fact she's a teenager. I hope I'm loving her without thinking of myself. I try to love her like I love a night filled with stars."

Joanna, age 51, mother of thirteen-year-old

"My mother brings love into our daily lives through talking and spending time together."

Cathy, age 17

"I feel love's presence in nature, and whenever I see something really beautiful."

Nyah, age 12

"The way I survive the teen years is by preaching less and listening more. No topic is off limits. My girls both know that I try not to judge what they say to me."

mother of two teen girls

"My mother is like a student of our family—of our dreams, needs, wants, and desires. She makes our house filled with love. She is always saying love is very important and surrounding yourself with people who feel the same way is also important if you want to find happiness."

Ryan, age 18

*T*here are plenty of times when we find it difficult to connect with our daughters. For whatever reason, there are communication barriers between us that we cannot seem to overcome. When these impasses happen, we can surmount them by responding with *unconditional* love, a concept that our daughters may understand better than we do.

"Unconditional love is when someone loves me like God or my mother no matter what I do."

Brie, age 10

"Unconditional love is how I love my dog and my dog loves me. We don't show it to each other. We just love each other."

Hillary, age 11

"I feel God's unconditional love when I pray."

Jennifer, age 13

"My mommy gives me unconditional love."

Meg, age 15

"I feel love for all the good parts and all the bad parts of my mom when we listen to music together or go for quiet walks."

Sarah, age 11

Almost every girl who answered the question "What is unconditional love?" defined it, and believes it exists. Additionally, girls understand that unconditional love is not the same as romantic love, with its possessiveness, intensity, and often transitory nature. Whatever their differences in religious practice, self-awareness, or perception of spirituality, from ages eight to eighteen, girls have faith in unconditional love and find their faith comforting. Adolescent girls want to be loved unconditionally and want to love back in the same way, even if they do not think they are capable of it.

How might you define unconditional love for your daughter?

TO ME, UNCONDITIONAL LOVE IS . . .

How might your daughter define unconditional love?

I THINK YOU WOULD SAY THAT UNCONDITIONAL
LOVE IS WHEN . . .

"I try to not blame or guilt-trip her about who she is
or what she does. I work at loving her without judging her every action or controlling her except for
her own safety."

Francine, age 38, mother of twelve-year-old

"When we are having an argument, and she says,
'I hate you, Mother,' I love her. When she's late to be
picked up and I'm sitting in the car stewing, I love
her. When she slams the door in my face, I love her."

Anne, age 49, mother of daughter, age 15

"She is the love of my life. She is my angel. There are times when I don't like her. Sometimes I ask myself, 'Who is this girl?' But I love her—even the girl I don't know."

Sally, age 51, mother of daughter, age 17

"I affirm her exerting of independence, her abilities, her confidence, her 'space.' I try not to personalize it when she shows she dislikes me. I never give up loving her even when she is difficult."

Victoria, age 44, mother of daughter, age 15

"Is there a way to give her total self-confidence in life by just loving her no matter what? I hope so."

Sheila, age 37, mother of daughter, age 14

"First I must be in tune with myself. That means I'm feeling confident, generous, and good about myself. I'm not beating myself up about anything. Then I am able to love them the same way."

Kelly, age 42, mother of daughters ages 13, 15

"I acknowledge what is important to her even if I disagree. I try to teach her to love herself so she can create a life for herself that she loves, not the one I think she will love."

Laurie Ann, age 40, mother of daughter, age 16

"My daughters are my gift to the world, and God's gift to me."

Jean, age 60, mother of daughters ages 25, 27, and 31

"Unconditional love is what I feel for my children. It does not require that they love me or I love them. It's just there. Love."

Margaret, age 35, mother of two, ages 6 and 11

"I don't think you can love your daughter totally until you love yourself, both the good parts and the bad parts."

Yolanda, age 37, mother of daughter, age 15

List some ways that you demonstrate your unconditional love to your daughter:

I SHOW MY UNCONDITIONAL LOVE FOR YOU
WHEN I . . .

Unconditional love is not possessive. It transcends all faiths. However, most of us love conditionally. We get into trouble when we expect a "return" on our love. We become "hurt" when someone we love does not love us back "enough," or takes our love for granted, or simply loses interest in loving us as much as we would like. Conditional love is judgmental. As parents, we should try not to judge our daughters' behavior and then dole out our love as either punishment or reward.

"I am fifteen, but I feel a lot older. I've been feeling very alone lately. There is no way I can please my parents. I know my mother thinks I'm ugly, because she's always on me to lose weight. She's right, but I can't do anything about it. I guess I've given up. My dad is always cracking jokes about me being fat. I know he means well, but it hurts."

Adrian, age 16

"I have a problem and it's that I don't have anyone. My mom and my stepdad are very strict and it seems like no matter what I do to try to be like they want me to, I get yelled at. Even if I do all my chores perfectly."

Pricilla, age 14

"I need to find out who my true self is, because around my parents I can't be myself because I'm supposed to be perfect, which I'm not."

Christie, age 11

"Every day my thoughts of myself get smaller and smaller because of things that my sister and brother

say about me. My mom and dad won't tell them to
stop. I don't know where to turn.

Candice, age 12

Moreover, there are plenty of times when we feel *no*
love, conditional or unconditional. For instance, I am running late, find a parking place, put my turn signal on to indi-
cate that that parking place is mine, but then someone slips
their car in before I get to it. It is hard to feel love for that
person. Or, when, after a long day, I come home to find that
the dog got into the garbage, which is now strewn all over
the living room, it is hard, at that moment, to love the dog.
Yet, much of the time we find great satisfaction and joy in
loving and being loved conditionally in a variety of ways. We
love people, places, things, and ideas.

I feel romantic love for my husband; caring and compassionate love for my daughters and for my closest women
friends; devotional love for my parents, sister, and her sons;
loving-kindness for my community; nostalgic love for places
with special meaning for me like Nantucket and the mountains of Utah. When I am honest with myself, I know that I
set conditions on these feelings and often use my controlling ways to try to experience them on demand. On the

other hand, I feel grateful that I have so many parts to my life that I am able to love, even conditionally.

What people and places do you love and how do you love them?

I LOVE . . .

We also love activities, objects, and ideas, and pass many of these loves on to our daughters, just as our mothers and grandmothers passed their loves on to us. When handed down from generation to generation, these loves may be transformed into passions, enthusiasms, simple pleasures, or rejected altogether, but they still originated as love. From my grandmother Geneal, I inherited a love of opera, drama, gardening, all things having to do with the countries of Greece and India, occasional outrageous breaches of decorum, and a deep and abiding belief in the mystery and magic of everyday life. From my grandmother Lola, I inherited a love of baking, healing, children, practicality, and the Western desert. And from my mother I inherited a love of hospitality, ritual, literature, travel, and, I must confess, sweaters.

What specific activities, things, or ideas were passed down to you from generations of women in your family that you have incorporated into your own life?

I INHERITED A LOVE FOR . . . FROM . . .

What loves have you passed on to your daughter?

LIKE ME, YOU LOVE . . .

Our greatest challenge in parenting is to go beyond loving conditionally to unconditional love. As little children,
unconditional love is the only way we know how to relate to
our world. We trust in the world and we live in the moment.
We let love happen.

We don't try to understand or identify our experiences,
but instead simply trust in them. We love unconditionally
because we were born loving unconditionally, and there has
not been time yet to experience otherwise. We are filled
with wonder.

"I remember being a little kid at this one family re-union, and watching my cousins slide down a banis-ter. Then we all crowded onto one porch swing with olives on each of our fingers and watched my grand-father grill chicken. I loved everyone there, and they loved me. The whole memory glows."

Rhoda, age 46, mother of two girls, ages 8 and 12

"When I was very little, my mother used to take me on walks through the orange groves and we would eat fresh oranges, and she would make up funny sto-ries. We would laugh and laugh. That was the only time I can think of that I felt unconditional love."

Patrice, age 51, mother of three girls, ages 11, 14, and 19

"My aunt was teaching me my colors and numbers and she was so patient and loving. It seemed like she was the only one who had time for me. I was number six out of seven children. The best part was that she didn't care whether I learned them or not."

Jean, age 52

"We lived with my grandmother when I was a young child. My parents were very strict about me taking a nap every afternoon for two hours, but when my grandmother took care of me, she'd let me play under the covers instead. Or she'd lie next to me and we'd talk. I loved her so much, and she loved me."

Hilary, age 32

"My earliest memory is being with my mother in our barn. She was taking care of a new baby calf. Maybe it was the light, but I remember it as magical. I was surrounded by all this love and I loved everything surrounding me back."

Taylor, age 55

Describe someone who loved you unconditionally when you were a young child.

I WAS LOVED UNCONDITIONALLY BY . . .

As Celeste Snowber Schroeder writes, "Love requires not a one time of becoming, but an ongoing surrender into the womb of God." The idea of an "ongoing surrender" implies we must make time in our lives for unconditional love; time we cannot preprogram. How frustrating. We are far too busy to experience an ongoing surrender into love. Who can sandwich in an hour for unconditional love if, directly after eight hours of work, not including travel time, we pick up the cleaning and a prescription for head lice, and then start the evening off trying to put together some sort of chicken, cheese, and vegetable concoction and conduct a vocabulary drill in French at the same time?

Plus, we are not good at "ongoing surrender into the

womb of God." Instead of simply letting go and surrendering, we look for activities that will direct our surrender. We are still in control mode. I have spent many years filling my time with activities such as yoga, walking on the beach, jogging, and several different meditative practices, all of which I still enjoy doing (the key word here) on a regular basis. I kept hoping one of them would be the activity that would result in a "surrender into the womb of God" experience. None of them worked. Ultimately, the stillness required before writing prayers for my daughters did. I learned that I could do nothing but be still. When I completely surrendered, love (and the words of a prayer) happened.

Yet the yearning of our inner self to love and be loved unconditionally is always present no matter what role we play, mother or daughter. When our daughters do not get unconditional love, they blame themselves. Fear of rejection from conditional love of others makes them defensive, living life in a crouch. One of my favorite children's classics, *A Wrinkle in Time,* by Madeleine L'Engle, begins with a portrait of the heroine, thirteen-year-old Meg, in her attic bedroom. With unruly "mouse-brown hair," "a mouth full of teeth covered with braces," and eyeglasses, Meg considers herself "a monster." She ruminates on how she does everything wrong; on how she is "too abrasive," "dumb," "a baby," and "a delinquent." Angry at the world, she finds herself unable to love, and unlovable. Meg and her companions experience many fantastic adventures and meet a number of mythical creatures in order to rescue her father, who is being held captive in another galaxy by IT, the essence of evil.

At the end of the story, Meg must fight IT to rescue her little brother, and she must perform this task alone, armed only with her inner resources. During the confrontation, when faced with death, she suddenly realizes that there is only one weapon that will defeat the all-powerful loathing and hatred of IT, and that weapon is love. In a flash Meg becomes aware that she *is* lovable, and that during her adventures she has met many people who love her, including her parents, her three brothers, and a good friend. She then feels such deep love for her brother that ultimately she is able to rescue them both, and is transformed from a self-doubting, angry child to a courageous young woman filled with joy and love.

Whatever problems, confusions, crises, or self-doubts our daughters experience, they, like Meg, are transformed by unconditional love. It is when we are lovingly present for our daughters without any assumptions about what we expect from ourselves or them that this transformation takes place. During these times we are not relating to our daughters to fill some need of our own or to demonstrate our ability as good mothers. We are surrendering to our love for her and her love for us. Experiencing unconditional love is something all of us yearn for and are capable of. We can allow this compassionate, nonjudgmental love to occur between us every day of our lives. When it does occur, it closes the circle, connecting us for a lifetime.

I Trust That I'll Find

The love that is mine
Generous, trusting, and pure.
It waits in my soul,
It's what makes me whole,
It's the answer, the key, and the cure.

I hope that someday
I can share in some way
The love grown inside me from birth.
For the love that I grow
Is a gift that I know
I'll give back as I give to this earth.

MORE PRAYERS ON MY PILLOW

TO

FROM YOUR MOTHER, WHO LOVES YOU
UNCONDITIONALLY

Resources

BOOKS

Spiritual Poetry/Writing

Astrov, Margot, editor. *The Winged Serpent: American Indian Prose and Poetry*. Beacon Press, 1974. The best collection of Native American spiritual writing I have read.

Cameron, Julia. *The Artist's Way: A Spiritual Path to Higher Creativity*. Tarcher Putnam, 1992. The gold standard in self-empowerment, spiritual writing, and creativity.

Cerwinske, Laura. *Writing as a Healing Art*. Penguin Putnam Inc, 1999. An exceptionally honest book about writing and journaling.

Cotner, June. *Mothers and Daughters: A Poetry Celebration*. Harmony Books, 2001. A beautiful collection of poetry written by mothers and daughters about their relationships.

Martin, William. *The Parent's Tao Te Ching*. Marlowe and Company, 1999. An absolute must for parenting, poetry, and spirituality. This is probably the most inspirational poetry book on spiritual parenting ever written.

Nye, Naomi Shihab. *This Same Sky: A Collection of Poems from around the World*. Aladdin Paperbacks, 1996. Another compilation of poetry that is exceptional because it is international in scope.

Straus, Celia. *Prayers on My Pillow: Inspirations for Girls on the Threshold of Change.* Ballantine, 1998. For girls ages 10–17.

———. *More Prayers on My Pillow: Words of Comfort and Hope for Girls on the Journey to Self.* Ballantine, 2000. For girls ages 13–21.

Sacred Space/Circles/Altars

Carnes, Robin Deen, and Sally Craig. *Sacred Circles: A Guide to Creating Your Own Women's Spirituality Group.* Harper San Francisco, 1998. The definitive and, as far as I know, only book on how to create sacred circles for women.

McMann, Jean. *Altars and Icons: Sacred Spaces in Everyday Life.* Chronicle Books, 1998. A beautifully photographed book of personal altars with lots of good ideas.

Streep, Peg. *Altars Made Easy.* Harper San Francisco, 1997. The most complete and clear book on making altars.

Wright, Wendy. *Sacred Dwelling.* Crossroad Publishers, 1989. A comprehensive book on sacred places in our lives.

Faith/Spirituality

Anderson, Sherry Ruth, and Patricia Hopkins. *The Feminine Face of God.* Bantam, 1991. A masterpiece of journalism and spirituality that chronicles the authors' search for women who have been empowered by their Divinity.

Beck, Charlotte Joko. *Nothing Special: Living Zen.* HarperCollins, 1995. A wonderful book about Zen written by a master teacher.

Brussat, Frederic and Mary Ann. *Spiritual Literacy: Reading the Sacred in Everyday Life.* The complete guide to spirituality in everyday life, organized in accessible, fun ways.

Chinmoy, Sri. *A Child's Heart and a Child's Dreams.* Aum Publications, 1986. A beautiful little book about children's spirituality, filled with wisdom.

Davis, Patricia H. *Beyond Nice: The Spiritual Wisdom of Adolescent Girls.* Fortress Press, 2001. Breaks new ground on this topic. A great read.

Eagle, Brooke Medicine. *Buffalo Woman Comes Singing.* Ballantine, 1991. Offers an incredible insight into the spiritual life of Native Americans with poetic prose.

Hanh, Thich Nhat. *The Heart of the Buddha's Teaching.* Broadway Books, 1999. Any book by this amazing poet and author is worth reading.

Hoffman, Enid. *Huna: A Beginner's Guide.* Whitford Press, 1976. A little-known author who writes incredible books about the Huna and the three selves.

Ingerman, Sandra. *Soul Retrieval: Mending the Fragmented Self.* Harper-Collins, 1991. Fascinating approach to finding the inner self.

May, Robert M. *Physicians of the Soul: The Psychologies of the World's Greatest Spiritual Teachers.* Crossroad Press, 1982. The best overview of the world's spiritual teachers, from Jesus to Krishna.

Norris, Kathleen. *Amazing Grace.* Riverhead Books, 1998. Anything by this author is enriching and rewarding.

Rolheiser, Ronald. *The Holy Longing: The Search for a Christian Spirituality.* Doubleday, 1999. An inspirational book about how one discovers spirituality and integrates it into everyday life.

Smith, Robert Lawrence. *The Quaker Book of Widsom.* Eagle Brook (William Morrow), 1998. A beautifully written book overviewing the Quaker faith.

Chogym, Trungpa. *Shambhala: The Sacred Path of the Warrior.*

Shambhala, 1988. If you're interested in Buddhism, this author is compassionate, caring, and accessible.

Zukav, Gary. *The Seat of the Soul.* Fireside Books (Simon and Schuster), 1990. A classic.

Spiritual Parenting

Boyer, Jr., Ernest. *Finding God at Home.* Harper and Row, 1988. Well worth reading and practical, too.

Cavaletti, Sofia. *The Religious Potential of the Child.* Liturgy Training Publication, 1992. A beautiful insight into the soul of a child.

DeMello, Anthony. *The Way to Love.* New York: Doubleday, 1991. Parenting insight that is both spiritual and practical

Doe, Mimi. *The Ten Principles of Spiritual Parenting.* HarperCollins, 1998. A classic that I use all the time. Anything by Mimi is terrific and practical. Visit her Web site (see page 279)

——. *Busy but Balanced: Practical and Inspirational Ways to Create a Closer, Calmer Family.* St. Martin's, 2001. Organized by season. Filled with hundreds of ways to spiritually parent.

Fitzpatrick, Jean Grasso. *Something More.* Viking Penguin, 1991. A beautiful book on spirit and parents.

Kabat-Zinn, Myla and Jon. *Everyday Blessings: The Inner Work of Mindful Parenting.* New York: Hyperion, 1997. A classic on spiritual parenting that is personal and practical as well.

L'Engle, Madeleine. *Trailing Clouds of Glory: Spiritual Values in Children's Books.* Westminster Press, 1985. A little-known book that is out of print, but if you can get it, it is a treasure trove of good advice and sound suggestions on books for your daughters.

Linthorst, Ann Tremaine. *Mothering as a Spiritual Journey.* Crossroads Publishing, 1993. A most beautifully written and inspirational book on spiritual mothering.

McDaniel, Bonnie W. *In the Eye of the Storm: A Celebration of Family and the Real Purpose of Home.* AGL Press, 1999. A wonderful book of ideas on how to connect with your children through activities centered in the home.

Robbins, Patience. "The Call to Spiritual Growth in Parenthood," *The Shalem News,* 1997.

Prather, Hugh and Gayle. *Spiritual Parenting.* Three Rivers Press, 1996. Another classic on spiritual parenting that is funny and accessible.

Schroeder, Celeste Snowber. *In the Womb of God.* Triumph Books, 1989. A beautiful book on pregnancy and spirituality.

Vannoy, Steven W. *The 10 Greatest Gifts I Give My Children.* Fireside Books, 1994. An accessible and practical how-to-parent book.

Parenting

Alexander, Debra Whiting. *Loving Your Teenage Daughter Whether She Likes It or Not.* New Harbinger Publications, 2001. This one is a must because it is filled with good advice and is organized by topic in a way you can use instantly.

Dodson, Shireen, and Teresa Barker. *The Mother-Daughter Book Club.* Harper Perennial, 1997. A story of how mothers started a book club for their nine-year-old daughters, and how you can do the same.

Eagle, Carol J., and Carol Colman. *All That She Can Be.* Fireside, 1994. How you can recognize the warning signs of falling self-esteem and what you can do about it.

Firman, Julie, and Dorothy Firman. *Daughters and Mothers: Healing the Relationship.* Crossroad Publishers, 1990. Commonwealth Printing, 1989. A classic, particularly if you are trying to connect with your own mother as well as your daughter.

Gilligan, Carol, Nona Lyons, and Trudy J. Hammer. *Making Connections: The Relational Worlds of Adolescent Girls at Emma Willard School.* Harvard University Press, 1989. Another classic in the study of the inner selves of teenage girls.

Johnson, Andrea. *Girls Speak Out.* The Horn Book, 1999. A guide to self-esteem that tells you how to create your own "speak-out" sessions.

Leboyer, Frederick. *Birth without Violence.* Healing Arts Press, 1995. (Originally published in France in 1974.) The best book I have ever read about birth.

Mann, Judy. *The Difference.* Warner, 1996. Explores how parents, schools, and community teach girls to value themselves less.

Ohye, Bonnie. *Love in Two Languages.* Viking Press, 2001. An insightful book about teenage body language.

Orenstein, Peggy. *School Girls, Young Women, Self-Esteem, and the Confidence Gap.* Anchor Books, Doubleday, 1994. Another classic work on teenage girls.

Pipher, Mary. *Reviving Ophelia: Saving the Selves of Adolescent Girls.* Ballantine Books, 1994. A classic that many mothers of teenage girls have actually read.

Ponton, Lynn. *The Sex Lives of Teenagers.* Plume, 2001. A new book that addresses the realities of teenage sexuality.

Roffman, Deborah. *Sex and Sensibility: The Thinking Parent's Guide to Talking Sense About Sex.* Perseus Books, 2000. This is the best book I've read about how to talk about sex to your daughter.

Sachs, Brad G. *The Good Enough Child.* Quill, 2001. A wonderful book on why, as parents, we must be wary of nurturing perfectionism in our children.

Shure, Myrna B., and Roberta Israeloff. *Raising a Thinking Preteen: The "I Can Problem Solve" Program for 8 to 12 Year Olds.* Owl Books, 2001. A helpful book on preteens.

Taffel, Ron, and Melinda Blau. *The Second Family: How Adolescent Power Is Challenging the American Family.* St. Martin's, 2001. A book about teenagers and their peers versus family.

Self-Empowerment

Barach, Roland. *Mindtraps: Unlocking the Key to Investment Success.* Van K. Tharp, Associates, 1996. I know it may seem odd putting a book about investing into a spiritual parenting resource section, but there are eighty-plus "mindtraps" that Barach addresses, all of which could be applied to parenting as well as trading the markets. . . . Empowering because you understand that human nature is the same no matter what area in life you are attempting to succeed.

Haddock, Frank Channing. *Power of Will.* Robert Collier Publications, 1925. Haddock writes some of the most original thoughts about self-empowerment.

Katie, Byron. *Loving What Is: Four Questions That Can Change Your Life.* Harmony Books, 2002. A life-changing book that forces you to rethink how you perceive reality and truth. An excellent parenting tool.

Ford, Debbie. *The Dark Side of the Light Chasers: Reclaiming Your Power, Creativity, Brilliance, and Dreams.* Riverhead Books, 1998.

A hard and truthful look at what makes us behave in self-destructive ways.

Ruiz, Don Miguel. *The Four Agreements: A Toltec Wisdom Book.* Amber-Allen Publishing, 1997. A classic.

Salt, J. S., editor. *Always Accept Me for Who I Am.* Three Rivers Press, 1999. For boys and girls, 12–16. A collection of letters from teenagers on acceptance to their parents.

Shinn, Florence Scovel. Anthology of works, including *The Game of Life and How to Play It,* and *Your Word Is Your Wand.* De Vross and Company, 1988. A collection of Shinn's best works.

Ueland, Brenda. *If You Want to Write: A Book About Art, Independence and Spirit.* Greywolf Press, 1987. Ueland wrote this book in 1938, and it is my favorite book about how to live a creative and integrated life. Don't be put off by the reference to writing in the title.

Zweig, Connie, and Steve Wolf. *Romancing the Shadow: A Guide to Soul Work for a Vital, Authentic Life.* Ballantine Wellspring, 1997. The best book I've read on our dark sides.

Environment and Spirit

Butterfly Hill, Julia. *The Legacy of Luna: The Story of a Tree, a Woman and the Struggle to Save the Redwoods.* Harper San Francisco, 2000. For girls and boys, ages 10–18. An inspirational and exciting story of Butterfly Hill's two-year stay at the top of a redwood tree in a standoff with loggers.

Miller, Gordon. *Wisdom of the Earth: Visions of an Ecological Faith.* Green Rock Press, 1997. Beautiful combination of photography and faith-based text.

Streep, Peg. *Spiritual Gardening.* Time-Life Books, 1999. A beautiful and comprehensive book on gardening with spirit. Lots of good ideas for spiritual space.

Williams, Terry Tempest. *Refuge.* Vintage Books, 1991. Anything by this author is wonderful. This is about Williams's relationship with her mother, who is dying from cancer, and her struggle to save a desert bird sanctuary in Utah.

Healing through Spirit

Barasch, Marc Ian. *Healing Dreams.* Riverhead Books, 2000. A comprehensive book on how to interpret our dreams and how to use them to heal.

Cloud, Dr. Henry. *Changes That Heal.* Zondervan Publishing (HarperCollins), 1992. A faith-based book dealing with two concepts of grace and truth and how to use them to heal ourselves.

Dossey, Larry. *Prayer Is Good Medicine.* Harper San Francisco, 1996. Anything by Dossey is wonderful.

Goleman, Daniel, editor. *Healing Emotions: Conversations with the Dalai Lama on Mindfulness, Emotions, and Health.* Shambhala, 1997. A dialogue that is filled with wonderful insights from the Dalai Lama.

The Shalem Institute for Spiritual Formation

Tilden Edwards:

Living in the Presence: Spiritual Exercises to Open Our Lives to the Awareness of God. Harper San Francisco, 1971. An excellent book on how to enhance our own spirituality.

Living Simply through the Day: Spiritual Survival in a Complex Age. Paulist Press, 1973. Spiritual guidance in our busy world that is practical and profound.

Sabbath Time: Understanding and Practice for Contemporary Christians. Upper Room Books, 1992. This is an excellent book on how to create peace and spirituality in the home.

Dr. Gerald May:

The Awakened Heart: Opening Yourself to the Love You Need. Harper San Francisco, 1993. About love, and it is wonderful.

Simply Sane: The Spirituality of Mental Health. Crossroad Publishers, 1999. A fine book about spirituality and your emotions.

PARENTING WEB SITES AND ONLINE NEWSLETTERS

Aauw.org—American Association of University Women. This site is for all mothers and daughters in that they promote education and equality for both.

Academic.org—This site by the Women's College Coalition has tips for mothers and daughters to help girls fulfill their potential. Has a great list of math camps, science camps, and women's colleges.

Chelseahouse.com—Publisher carrying dozens of biographies of famous women, including African Americans, Hispanics, Asians, Native Americans.

Empoweredparenting.com—A wonderful site for parenting information.

Girlsinc.org—The fifty-year-old national youth organization "helping every girl become strong, smart and bold." Girls 6–18 can join in over one thousand locations with a focus on minority and economically at risk girls.

LifelongLearning—Empowerment.

Mentoring.org—The best site for mentoring.

Momalone.com news—For single moms.

Newmoon.org/network/index.html—Magazine for mothers and other adults to help girls grow up self-confidently.

Nwhp.org—National Women's History Project. This site has books, guides, posters, and lots of other materials to make women's history come alive for your daughter. It profiles numerous women's history projects around the country and also has a great list of links for other women's history sites.

Parentingteens.com—A great site for parenting teens.

RADdaily—Raising daughters today.

Raisingadaughter.com—Valerie Zilinsky's terrific site on how to parent a daughter from ages 1–21.

RASdaily.com—Raising sons today.

Spiritualparenting.com—Mimi Doe's Web site, which has a weekly newsletter. One of the best.

Spiritualparenting.com's weekly newsletter—Comes out on Thursdays. Excellent.

Storknet.com—One of the best sites for parenting young children to teens.

Soulretrieval.com—A terrific resource for journeying and empowerment by Pat Homeyer.

NEWSLETTER

"Echoes—Catechesis in the Family." An excellent newsletter about how parents can enjoy and nurture their children's relationship with God. Published by the Center for Children and Theology, Mount Rainier, Maryland.

ONLINE TEEN MAGAZINES AND WEB SITES

Bluemoon.com—An online magazine written for and by young teenagers.

Cyberteens.com—Written and designed by teens. Creativity, education.

Girlpower.com—Girls chat and share opinions and poetry.

Girlprayers.com—My site, where girls and mothers send requests for prayer-poems for specific problems.

Girlscouts.org—Great site about helping girls to develop their confidence and self-esteem.

Girlsite.com—Another good place to hang out for "tweens."

Girlslife.com—Another good site for young teenage girls with lots of activities to choose from.

GirlTech.com—One of the best sites I've come across for activities, creative opportunities, and interactivity for young teen girls.

Girlzone.com—A fun site for young "tweens" with lots of activities and self-confidence builders.

Gurl.com—A hip interactive site with lots of relevant games, contests, and relationship tips for girls.

Health.org/gpower/girlarea—Another welcoming and confidence-building site for teenage girls.

Teenvoices.com—Focuses on self-empowerment and on reaching goals.

ORGANIZATIONS

The Shalem Institute for Spiritual Formation
5430 Grosvenor Lane
Bethesda, Maryland 20814
Phone: 301-897-7334
Web site: www.shalem.org

Interfaith Conference of Metropolitan Washington
1419 V Street, NW
Washington, D.C. 20009
Phone: 202-234-6300

TELEVISION PROGRAMS FOR "TWEENS"

As Told by Ginger—Nickelodeon
Cyberchase—PBS
Lizzie McGuire—Disney Channel
Malcolm in the Middle—Fox
Zoom—PBS

SPOKEN WORD AND MUSIC

I'm More Than What I Seem—Spoken-word CD of prayer-poems from *Prayers on My Pillow* for adolescent girls recorded by celebrity women and their daughters, such as Annette Bening, Judith Ivey, and Kathleen Turner. Poetry, music, and book all-in-one. Produced by Padma Projects, Boston, Massachusetts.

About the Author

Celia Straus is a nationally known writer and speaker on adolescent girls and mother-daughter relationships. In 1998, Celia wrote *Prayers on My Pillow: Inspiration for Girls on the Threshold of Change*. She subsequently authored a sequel, *More Prayers on My Pillow*, and a spoken word CD of poetry, *I'm More Than What I Seem*, expressing the inner voice of teen girls. Her monthly relationship columns and daily inspirational messages are carried by leading parenting Web sites. As a scriptwriter of television documentaries and educational programming for video and interactive media, she has garnered over one hundred industry awards. A graduate of Mary Washington College of University of Virginia with a Masters degree from Georgetown University, Celia lives in Washington, D.C., with her husband and two teenage daughters. Visit her Web sites: www.girlprayers.com and www.motherdaughtercircle.com.

About the Artist

Julia Straus, daughter of Celia Straus, is a sophomore at Princeton University, where she hopes to pursue her study of history and art and continue to row on the Princeton Lightweight Crew Team. She was born in Washington, D.C., where she attended the Maret School for thirteen years.